"Are We There Yet?"

To order additional copies of

"Are We There Yet?"—
A Practical Guide to Sane Parenting,
by Marjorie Burch Brothers, call

1-800-765-6955.

Visit us at www.rhpa.org for more information on
Review and Herald products.

"Are We There Yet?"

A Practical Guide to Sane Parenting

Marjorie Burch Brothers, Ed.D.

REVIEW AND HERALD® PUBLISHING ASSOCIATION
HAGERSTOWN, MD 21740

This book was
Edited by Jeannette R. Johnson
Designed by Bill Kirstein
Cover illustration by Ralph Butler
Typeset: 13/15 Janson

PRINTED IN U.S.A.

02 01 00 99 98   10 9 8 7 6 5 4 3 2 1

R&H Cataloging Service
Brothers, Marjorie Burch
    "Are we there yet?" A practical
guide to sane parenting.

    1. Parent and child.   I. Title.

        306.874

ISBN 0-8280-1286-5

Dedication

To Greg
and Jana

Acknowledgments

I especially want to thank the many parents and children who have enriched and enlivened my life. Without your help and encouragement, this book would not have been possible.

Parts of some of the chapters in this book were previously published as magazine articles in "The Parents' Page" of *Signs* magazine. To those pastors who wrote, asking for permission to reprint these articles in church newsletters, a special thank-you. It was you who inspired me to keep on writing and to gather them into a book.

Contents

CHAPTER 1

Raising
Good Kids

C hris and Robin were tense when they brought their child, Lisa, into the kindergarten room, whispering that they had to see me before she started school. She had a problem they needed to tell me about. I had scheduled a parents' meeting the day before school started. Chris and Robin planned to stay for the meeting, so I agreed to talk with them right after the meeting.

All through my presentation I wondered about Lisa. There was certainly nothing visibly wrong with this child. She seemed delightful. She sat quietly during what must have seemed a long meeting, and every time I glanced in her direction she blinked a please-like-me smile at me. By the time the meeting was over I liked her. Whatever the problem was, I was certain we could conquer it together.

When the last parent had left the room, I was ready to talk with Chris and Robin. They clutched each other in their anxiety as they told me their problem. "Lisa picks her nose," they said.

I had planned to be very professional about this. Instead, I laughed. "But they *all* pick their noses," I told them.

Well, maybe there are some 5-year-olds who have never picked their noses. My point is that many parents of delightful children worry about things that are a natural part of a child's growing up. They worry about their child's eating habits, friends, and the stories they hear on the nightly news programs. *Will my child be safe?* they wonder. *Will he or she turn out OK?*

All children do some things that make their parents very proud. At other times they do things their parents wish they didn't do. But when does such behavior cease being a normal part of growing up and become a major problem? When should parents seek professional help?

This book is intended for those parents who are raising what I hesitate to call "average" children—very special children to the people who know them, but who fit in neither extreme of the behavior scale. These children aren't dropping out of school, but neither are they straight A students. Their parents try to teach them good manners but are sometimes surprised to see how rude they can be. They have never been in serious trouble but their parents are concerned about some of their habits. As adults, they will be the good citizens that their parents are now, but in the meantime their parents worry. For lack of a better term, I'm calling these children "good kids," for that is what they are.

The suggestions I give are just that—suggestions. Children are all so uniquely different that no one solution works for everyone. Still, certain techniques have worked for many people. My suggestions are gleaned from 36 years of teaching in a public school, from my training as a teacher, from my experience in raising my two children, from the many parents I have asked about parenting, from my work in Sunday schools, Sabbath schools, and vacation Bible schools, and from the students I have queried about what works in raising children. The incidents and the people I describe are real, though I have changed their names to protect their privacy.

DEBUNKING SOME MYTHS

First, let me debunk a few myths. You've no doubt heard that a parent must always love the child, as if love is all you need. This is true if you define love as always acting in your child's best interests. But if you define love as being that wonderful feeling you had for your newborn when you first brought him or her home from the hospital, then love is not enough. Think back: When you spent long nights walking your colicky baby as he or she screamed in pain, you may not have felt quite so excited about parenting. When your teenager said that if you hadn't insisted she be in by 11:00 p.m. she wouldn't have gotten that speeding ticket, you'd likely agree that it takes more than wonderful feelings about your teens to be a successful parent.

Parenting is not easy. Most of the time it's hard work.

Another of today's myths is that it's harder to raise children than it used to be. The truth is that raising children has never been easy. In some ways it's easier than it was in earlier times; in other ways it's harder. Modern science has removed some of the problems that parents worried about in earlier generations, but it has brought problems of its own. Certainly there are more resources available today for parents of a handicapped child. These children used to be hidden away in attics. Now they go to school, and many go on to work successfully at meaningful jobs.

Today's medicine has made it easier for children too. Many of the childhood diseases that plagued earlier generations can now be controlled. I remember when the opening of school was delayed because of an outbreak of polio. People were dying from it, and no one knew the cause. My mother's generation worried about smallpox. Today these diseases can be controlled if children have their shots.

TODAY'S REALITY

The scope of the drug problem is greater now, but the problem isn't new. In the early days of our country, some of the over-the-counter patent medicines contained drugs that are illegal today. People took them and, not surprisingly, some got hooked on them. When I was in high school, the drug of choice was alcohol. It's still the drug of choice for teens. The problem is not new, but drug use is more common, and it's beginning at a younger age. It's also closer to where we live.

Years ago when we read about Hell's Kitchen, we knew that it was a long way away, so we didn't feel threatened by it. Now we read about crime in our own neighborhood, and we worry. Again, the problem hasn't changed. People still misuse drugs. But now younger children are using them, and the easy availability of drugs worries parents.

The violence in neighborhoods worries parents too. Again, this isn't new. In the early days of our country teachers were chosen for their ability to stop the attacks of older students. It was not uncommon for big boys in those country schools to beat up their teachers. So the violence hasn't changed, but now it's student against student, and with guns involved it's much scarier. (I'll have more to say about the danger of guns in a later chapter. For right now let me just say it's something that has made raising children harder.)

Many parents are raising children in very difficult circumstances. Terri works as a bank teller to support herself and her 7-year-old son. She doesn't earn enough to pay for child care, so her son is at home alone after school until she gets home. She worries about him.

Paula and John are having difficulty in meeting expenses. They have two boys in elementary school. Paula works as a domestic, but it isn't full-time work, and it doesn't pay very well. John was recently hospitalized. He's working again, but he didn't have insurance, and by the time the family makes a payment on the medical bills, there isn't much left.

Robert and Hanna are raising their grandchild, Billy, who is 5. Hanna's mother, in her 90s, also lives with the family. Robert works full-time, so money isn't the main problem. "There's just never enough time for everything," Hanna told me.

Elsie and Gordon have four children, three girls and a boy. They live in a crime-infested neighborhood, but their income is too low for them to afford to live in a better district.

Glen and Edith live in another tough neighborhood. Glen is a long-distance truck driver, gone so much that he seldom sees his daughters. Edith told me that Glen took the job so he could earn enough for the family to move to a better place.

Parents aren't having an easy time of it; however, in spite of the difficulties, they are coping. Even in very bad neighborhoods, many parents are raising good children.

How do they do it? I've asked some of these parents the same question. None offered a long discourse on successful parenting; none gave me words of wisdom. The usual response was a shrug or a quick laugh. "I didn't think I was doing all that well," or "It isn't easy," they said. Yet when we look at these successful parents, we see that they have much in common.

They know where their children are. Their homes are the center of neighborhood activity, for it is there that the children come to play.

They work to better their neighborhood. They join neighborhood associations. They know who the community leaders are and become community leaders themselves, if need be.

They accept their child as he or she is. They expect their child to work hard in school, but are not disappointed if he or she gets lower grades than the neighbor's kids. They encourage their childrens' hobbies and sports but do not demand perfection.

They help their child succeed in school. They know that if their child is to succeed in life, he or she must do well in school. They check to see that homework is done and that the child is in school regularly and on time.

They are involved in their child's school. They meet with teachers to discuss progress. They attend PTA or other parenting meetings. Those who can, volunteer to work as aides or tutors in the school.

They regulate the television in their home. Their children are taught to choose the best of what is available and to limit the number of hours they watch TV. If programming is unsuitable for children, the set is turned off.

They actively teach their moral values to their children. For these families, right or wrong is not a matter of convenience; it is a practice followed consistently. The successful parents I talked with were establishing guidelines and expecting their children to follow them.

They accept help when they need it. Jeana attended a school where I taught. She was bright, outgoing, and very successful in school. Her mother brought her to school early enough so that she could clean up in the school bathroom before the other students arrived. Jeana didn't want her classmates to know that her family was homeless. They lived in a van parked across the street from the school, so her mother sought help from the school to make Jeana's life a little more normal.

Some years ago a group of women discovered that a contributing factor for most high school girls who drop out of school is because they don't have the proper clothes to wear. These women founded a "clothes closet" where parents can take their children for free clothes. The service is confidential; there should be no stigma attached to being poor.

WIC, a nutrition program for mothers and young children, is another help. Parents wanting the best for their children use services such as these.

At this point I can almost hear someone say that the characteristics I have listed could also be applied to successful parents living in any circumstances, and that is true. Successful parents care about their children, and their children know it.

There is another point that I wish I could add—but I can't. I wish I could say that, having done all that they could, these good parents relax in the knowledge that they have done their best. They know that children make choices—sometimes wise, and sometimes bad. For parents, the pain of these bad choices is worsened when they blame themselves or ask, "Where did I go wrong?" Parents working in adverse conditions need to remind themselves that even in the best of circumstances some children do go wrong.

CHAPTER 2

Setting Limits

The Vista Bridge in North Portland spans a scenic ravine. Most people have probably seen one similar to it. Teachers in Portland, where I taught, use it to illustrate the need to set limits for children. We ask, "Would you send your child across the Vista Bridge if there were no railings? Would you go across yourself?" I have found that successful parents set limits and expect their children to follow them.

Did your children sometimes challenge the guidelines? Yes, of course they did! Kids want to see how firm the limits are. I have driven across the Vista Bridge in a heavy fog, so heavy that I couldn't see the railings. I found myself edging closer, looking for them. It was scary, but knowing where the limits were gave me a sense of security. Likewise, knowing what the limits are gives children a sense of security. They know that someone cares what they do.

I once taught an eighth grade boy who ran into serious trouble when he was in high school. Eventually he was sent to an alternative school. His classmates, whom I had also taught, often came back to see me and to keep me apprised of their progress. In speaking of this boy, many said, "His parents didn't care anything about him. They just let him do anything he wanted."

CHILDREN WANT GUIDELINES

Most parents agree on the need to set limits. The question is how to set them and where. Let me give some examples.

One of my personal joys is taking each of my grand-daughters shopping for school clothes before school begins. I have been cautioned by my daughter and my daughter-in-law to be sure to ask whether the child likes the clothes before buying them. "If she doesn't like it, she won't wear it," they said.

I certainly agree with the advice. However, I learned very early that styles have changed since I shopped for clothes for my own children—and even more since *I* was that age. Our tastes are radically different. Moreover, the older each girl gets, the more she knows what she wants. So I have solved my dilemma by sticking to what I call "Guidelines for Setting Guidelines." Here they are:

Examine your standards. Sometimes we stick to a standard because it's comfortable. It's the way our parents did things, or maybe we think the neighbors might criticize us if we are different. It's important to discover whether a standard is your own belief in what is right and wrong, or simply personal taste.

Girls always wore dresses when I was in school. I may look back and say that I like the way girls looked in dresses (ignoring how we looked in those old yearbooks), but are dresses a question of moral values? I don't think so. So I go along with my granddaughters' choices and will continue to do so unless those choices conflict with my sense of modesty. Then I will draw the line and refuse to buy the item.

Consider your child's safety. Anything that jeopardizes your child's safety must be off limits. If your child refuses to follow safety rules while riding a bike or driving a car, the bike or the car should be off limits for a while. In recent years gang-related clothing has become a problem. Some students insist that because they do not belong to gangs, wearing clothing similar to that worn by gang members is not a problem. They need to remember that gangs are everywhere. Gang members may resent a nonmember copying their style of dress and retaliate. Or your child may be mistaken for a gang member by a rival gang seeking revenge.

A high school teacher told me of an eighth grader whose academic skills were so above the requirements of his class that his teachers sent him to the nearby high school for some higher level courses. When he arrived on his first day, he was promptly taken home to change his shirt. Teachers were afraid that he might be mistaken for a member of a gang from a neighboring school, one that was at odds with some of their own students.

Consider the needs of your own household. It's reasonable to expect members of the family to clean up after themselves and to respect the rights of others living in the house. For example, children must learn to organize their time so that others can get into the bathroom before school. If two children share a bedroom, both must learn to share the space and the cleaning duties.

I found that my own children, as well as students in my classroom, were more willing to keep the place clean if they had some say in what needed to be done and what their part in the cleanup would be. Face it, some jobs just aren't that much fun. Rotating the jobs makes many children willing to do them; they know that next time they'll get a better job. For our family, sitting around the dining table and planning the next week's jobs worked well.

Consider your child's well-being. Your child needs proper nutrition and enough sleep. Getting a child to eat the right foods at the right time can be a challenge. It's frustrating to prepare a good meal which the children pick at, only to have them insist that they're hungry as soon as the dinner dishes are put away. Keeping mealtimes on a regular schedule, with no snacks between meals, may help. (Be careful with this if the children are very young. Their stomachs are so small that they may need to eat more often than an adult.) Serving desserts only on special occasions has helped some families.

Bedtime can be a problem. It's hard to get some children to bed—and even harder to get them up. Keep in mind that some people need more sleep than others. Your daughter may be more willing to go to bed if she has a toy to take along. Allowing your son to read or listen to a CD or a radio for a short time may help. As with eating, it's easier to establish good habits if you can set a routine. When it's nearing bedtime, let your son or daughter play in the bathtub for a while and then read or play quietly before going to bed.

At bedtime, some children learn to play games, "needing" one thing after another, keeping their parents busy long after they should be asleep. You may need to remind yourself who the parent is and tell your child, "No more drinks. It's time for you to go to sleep." Sometimes a night light helps.

Refuse to cave in when you know it's wrong. In a television news program teens were asked about a proposal to curb teen smoking, already illegal in the state where I live. One girl said that her mother has her smoke at home. "She knows that I'm going to smoke, and she doesn't want me to sneak around behind her back."

None of us want our child to hide things from us. I am concerned, however, that buying the cigarettes for teens—as another girl said her mother did—or smoking with them, is giving permission. Children often argue when their parents refuse permission, but they can also blame parents when things don't go right. And sometimes kids would rather tell their friends that their parents won't let them do something than admit to their friends that they don't feel comfortable doing it.

One mother told me of the time her high schooler, Jessica, asked permission to spend the weekend with a friend whose parents would be gone. The mother was uneasy about the arrangement, but both girls were reliable, and she hated to imply that she didn't trust Jessica. And even though the friend lived near enough so that Jessica could come home easily, the mom still hesitated. When she learned that the friend's brother would also be there, and that he was inviting a friend, this mother said no. She was surprised when Jessica thanked her. The girl had been uncomfortable about the situation also, but she didn't want to hurt her friend's feelings.

One other precaution: Be careful not to micromanage your child. Children grow up very quickly. Their lives take them out of your home fairly early, and they must make their own decisions, based on information you have given them. They need experience in making decisions. And they need to know that some decisions have poor consequences. Letting them make small choices from the first day they can will help them make wiser choices later.

CHAPTER 3

Keeping Your Child Safe

When I taught Billy in kindergarten, there was nothing in his life to predict his death two years later. His family fit the ideal for raising children. His parents loved each other and their two little boys. They lived on a farm near both sets of grandparents.

When Billy was in second grade, he stayed with his grandparents for a few days while his mother went to the hospital for surgery. On a crisp fall morning his uncle brought Billy's cousin over, and the boys went with their grandfather and the uncle to look over the winter wheat. The men left the boys in the pickup while they walked across the field.

Neither man thought that the gun in the rack behind the seat was loaded or they would have never left the boys alone. As Billy and his cousin got it out to look at it, it went off. Billy died in the same hospital where his mother was a patient.

The tragedy extended far beyond the sorrow over a

promising young life that was lost. It left a devastated family behind. I met Billy's parents recently. After more than 30 years, they still grieve for him.

Gun safety. In 1993 19 children were accidentally killed in my home state of Oregon. Nationally, 230 children are killed each year by unintentional shootings in the home, and an estimated 19,000 are hurt. The Center to Prevent Handgun Violence reports some startling findings:

• More than one third of all accidental shootings of children occur in the homes of friends or relatives.

• The risk of suicide is five times greater when there is a gun in the home.

• Depressed teens who commit suicide are more likely to use a gun than any other method.

Gun safety experts advise parents who own guns to lock the guns and the ammunition in separate places and to be sure that children do not have access to the keys. They also offer this advice:

• Stress to your children the danger of playing with a gun.

• Explain that gun violence in the movies and on TV is not real. Real guns *do* hurt people.

• Tell your children that if they are with friends who show them a gun, they are to leave immediately and report the incident to their parents and teachers.

Protect your own health. It's important for parents to protect their own health so that their child gets off to a healthy start. I once requested that the diagnostic center of the medical school in Portland do an evaluation of one of my students. Children who have been referred spend a week attending school there while they are being evaluated by a team of specialists. Teachers are invited to spend a day watching the process from a viewing room for visitors.

All the children we watched were having problems in their regular classrooms, but one child stood out from the others. He was unable to function with other children. He cried, wandered around, and finally had to be taken off by himself. We all asked about him. The supervisor said that they had been unable to find anything wrong with him— except that his mother was an alcoholic.

Childhood shots are important. Melvin started school in my kindergarten classroom. He was special to me, because he was the first child whose parent I had also taught. I felt as though I were a grandmother to him. I was deeply saddened when he had to be transferred to a special classroom in January—he had lost his hearing in a measles outbreak.

Although many childhood diseases have been conquered, they are still around. Children need to be protected.

Talk safety. Much of what I suggest about child safety involves education—telling your child what to do. I can almost hear parents saying, "We talk too much already. And what we say goes in one ear and out the other." But there is a lot of evidence to support that telling children what to do does work.

Each year firemen come to the public schools in Portland to talk with the students about fire safety. One of the things they emphasize is that if one's clothes catch fire, he or she is to "stop, drop, and roll."

"Running," they tell the students, "fans the flames. Rolling on the ground helps to smother the fire."

One fireman told the story of a young boy at a family backyard cookout. When his mother's clothes caught fire, she ran. The boy tackled her, football style, and rolled her on the ground until the fire was out.

A young girl accompanied her father to the family

cabin in the mountains, where they spent the day getting the cabin ready for the family vacation. The mother and the rest of the family planned to arrive later in the day. When the father had a heart attack that afternoon, the girl applied CPR until her mother arrived and could summon help.

The third incident involves a younger child. In one of those quiet little towns near where I live, a family took their 6-year-old to the movies. During the movie the boy went out to use the restroom. When a man tried to abduct him, the boy kicked, screamed, and raised such a fuss that his would-be abductor let go of him and rushed out of the theater. A theater attendant followed the man while another attendant called police. The police arrested the man, who was later convicted of abducting and murdering three other young boys in nearby towns.

My point is: Children *do* listen; they *do* follow our directions.

Now for some other safety suggestions:

If your car is moving, make sure that your child is securely fastened into a seat of the proper size. A seat that is too large or too small may be dangerous. Be alert for a possible recall of the seat you are using. Some companies report that only 10 percent of buyers bring in their car seats when a recall notice is sent out. Some of these seats may be worn out or no longer used, but some may still be in use. Notices may be posted in stores, in newspapers, or in your pediatrician's office. Look for them.

Never leave a child alone near water. If the telephone rings while you are bathing your child, take him or her along when you answer it—or let it ring. Children can drown in very little water. Some have drowned in fishponds or in toilet bowls. Keep the toilet lid down and the bathroom door closed if you have a young child in the house.

In my town drowning is the leading cause of accidental death in young children. Some parents use a safety vest for their child when they are at the beach, but safety experts advise this may not be enough. The greatest deterrent to an accidental drowning, they say, is an alert parent. Even reading a book while a child plays near the water may distract the parent long enough for the child to get in trouble.

Cover electrical outlets, and keep appliances away from places where they can fall into water. A blow-dryer or a toaster that falls into water can be a killer.

Check your child's toys for wheels, buttons, or eyes that can be pulled off and swallowed. The Consumer Product Safety Commission reports that emergency rooms treat more than 148,000 toy-associated injuries every year. In addition to choking on small parts, children have been injured by darts, arrows, and other objects with sharp points.

Safety pins are not toys, but children do swallow them. Many of these would do no damage if the pins were closed. An open safety pin usually sticks somewhere in the child's throat. Simply closing the safety pin before putting it away could eliminate this problem.

Fence off any areas which are unsafe for your child. Stairs, streets, swimming pools, or shops are hazardous for toddlers. One hospital emergency room reported that falls accounted for half of their unintentional injuries among children younger than 1 year. Most stores have posted a warning about leaving a child unattended in shopping carts, yet children still fall from them.

Keep your child with you when you are visiting in a place where you don't know the hazards. This is true, whether you are visiting in a home or in a public place.

Make sure your child's name is not visible on clothing. Strangers can more easily persuade a child to go along with them if they know the child's name. However, children are more often abducted or molested by someone they know than by a stranger.

Spend time talking and listening to your child. Listen especially for clues that your child is uncomfortable about something. Instruct your child to always let someone know where he or she is. Have them check in after school before going to play. Children should let the parent know where they are going and who they will be with. Then the parent will know where to start looking if they aren't back when they should be.

Be very careful with medications. In larger doses, even prescribed medicines may be dangerous for children. Be aware, too, that visiting grandparents often carry medicines in purses or traveling bags—medicines that can be lethal to children.

Check under sinks in your kitchen and bathrooms. Insecticides and many household cleaners are poisonous or caustic. Get stickers with "yucky" faces to identify these. Schools often give these out. Or you may be able to get them from your safety council. Even these are not enough for a very young child, however. If you have a young child in your house, keep all medicines and cleaning supplies in a cabinet, well out of reach. Grandparents have good intentions, but many of them haven't had young children around for a while. When you are visiting, ask them if you can put their cleaning supplies into a safe place. I have found the cupboard above the refrigerator to be the best place in our house.

Be sure that the smoke detectors are in working order. Set a definite time each year—such as New Year's

Day or when the time changes in the spring and fall—to check all of the detectors. Young children often hide when they are frightened and could succumb to smoke before they could be rescued. Smoke alarms give you more time. Teach your child to feel the door before opening it if the alarm goes off. Have a family plan of where to meet—outside—if there is a fire. And remember to teach them to "stop, drop, and roll" if their clothes catch fire.

Teach them what to do if they are lost. When I was a child, the standard advice was to find a police officer. That's still good advice if you live in a small town where the officer is always available. It's a good idea to teach any child that police officers like children and will help them. Sadly, some children have been scared by adults who threaten children by saying that the police will lock them up if they are bad. The officers who visit the Portland schools show handcuffs to the students and let them try them on. The handcuffs don't fit a child, and the police assure the students that they don't take children to jail.

However, most children don't have the option of telling a police officer that they're lost because they don't know where to find one. Many communities have a block home, or some similar program. Homes that have been checked out and deemed safe are marked with a sign in the window so that a child who is lost or in trouble can go there for help. These are especially helpful if the child is going to or coming from school.

Teach your children what the symbol looks like and what it means. (Many schools are doing this.) Perhaps you can walk through your neighborhood with your children and point out the signs. Check with your school to see whether there is a program like this in your area. If there isn't, consider starting one. If your neighborhood doesn't have this and your child must go to an unmarked house, teach him to stay on the porch while the person telephones for help.

If the child is lost or in trouble in a shopping area, it's a good idea to go to a store clerk for help. This person can call security or have a parent paged. Under no circumstances should the child go with a stranger—woman or man—for help.

Teach them the difference between "good secrets" and "bad secrets." Good secrets are fun things, such as a surprise birthday party or a Christmas present. Bad secrets are the kinds of things someone tells them not to tell their parents. Assure your children that they can tell you anything about things or people that scare them or make them feel uncomfortable. No one should tell them to keep a "bad" secret. Be sure your child knows that the parts of his or her body that are covered by a bathing suit are private and *no one* should ever touch them there. Teach them that they should tell you if someone touches them in a way they don't like.

Teach them not to pick up needles, balloons, or other trash that they find on the way to school or in other places. Instead, tell them to report their findings to an adult who will take care of such litter. In public restrooms they should not push the paper towel down in the wastebasket. Needle users sometimes put used needles there, and people have pricked themselves in this way.

Take a first aid training course. On a field near my house, lightning struck three young boys who were trying out for football. Two were seriously hurt. Both are now out of the hospital, and one is back on the playing field. Their parents knew how to give them CPR that, paramedics say, saved their lives.

LATCHKEY KIDS

I have some concerns about young children who go home after school to an empty house and stay alone until a parent gets home from work. Every state in the United States has laws forbidding leaving a child under a certain age alone. Though the age varies from state to state (in Oregon it's 10), most primary school teachers know of children who are alone for several hours after school. There are various reasons for this. Sometimes child care is not available or the parent simply cannot afford it. In some cases, schools and churches have established latchkey programs for these children. But there are never enough.

If your child must go home to an empty house, here are some safety precautions:

• Notify your child's teacher that he or she is home alone. If there is a storm, or if the child if frightened, someone can look after him.

• Ask a trustworthy neighbor to watch for the child. Arrange for the child to go there if he needs to.

• Teach your child that if the door is open, or there are other signs that the house has been broken into, not to go inside.

• Have your child telephone you as soon as he or she gets home.

• Have your child stay inside the house.

• Teach him or her to lock the door and to not answer the doorbell.

• Set up guidelines for answering the phone. If you have an answering machine, ask your child to listen for your voice before answering. Otherwise, program the machine to say that you will return the call; your child says nothing. If you don't have an answering machine, you and your child can devise a signal. For example, when you call, let the phone ring twice, hang up, and call again. Your child answers on the fourth ring. Under no circumstances should your child tell the caller that he or she is alone.

CHAPTER 4

Helping Your Child Do Well in School

I scarcely slept at all the night before our oldest child started school. I worried about him. Except for church functions, he had never before been anywhere alone. Questions tumbled through my mind as I tried to sleep. *Had we taught him everything he should know before he started school? Would his teacher be a good one? Would he be able to make friends?*

He looked so small and vunerable, standing there at the curb waiting for the van that would take him to kindergarten. But he was so happy and excited when the van arrived that the driver had to remind him that I wanted to take his picture by the school bus that first morning.

He got on the bus and didn't look back.

I look at that picture now and see his eager face and hear him telling me to hurry up so he can begin his big adventure. Then I remember that many parents are anxious about that first day of school. Even if your child has been in school for several years, the first day is still exciting.

But your concern for their doing well in school shouldn't end with that first bell of the new school year. Your home plays a crucial part in your child's success in school, and there are many ways you can help.

Stimulate your child's curiosity. An eagerness to learn is the one trait that will help your children most in doing well in school. Choose toys that ignite their curiosity, games that help them explore the world around them. Steer away from toys that allow them to watch without doing anything. For example, building blocks of all kinds spark your child's creativity; most windup toys do not.

Help your child develop guidelines for watching television. Choose programs that match your own values. Limit the time your child spends watching TV. Reliable studies indicate that children who do well in school watch less television than those who do not do as well.

Read to your child. Even after your child can read well himself, read to him, and let him read to you. Choose easy, fun books for recreational reading. If your child misses a few words on a page, say them, and let him or her go on. You'll find that your child picks up many of the words from the context, just as you do. Don't miss the meaning of the story by stopping to "sound out" words. You can save that for practice periods.

Visit your child's school. Get to know the teachers. Ask what your role in homework should be. Tell the teachers about your child's interests, both in and out of school. Listen to the teacher's suggestions. Be sure to make these visits often enough so that you aren't showing up only when there's a problem. Phoning ahead for an appointment will help you avoid a time when the teacher is too busy to meet with you.

Realize that regular attendance is important. A

child's attitude about school is formed early. If you are casual about the time your child arrives at school and about absences, your child may decide that school is not important. A school attendance officer tells me that students with a poor attendance record, whether from absences or tardiness, are more likely to drop out of school before graduating than are those students with a good record. The pattern begins early.

Be sure that your child is on time. Most children are early birds. They function best early in the morning. Many schools respond to this by scheduling the skill subjects early in the school day. You don't want your child to miss this instruction.

Be sure your child is fed and rested before school each morning. This means an early bedtime and a nourishing breakfast. According to one school nurse, many children don't like the traditional foods that Americans eat for breakfast. They are more likely to eat well if parents serve things the child likes; for example, spaghetti instead of oatmeal. A picky eater may eat better in a school breakfast program where she is with others her age. Ask whether your child's school has such a program.

Set aside a time and place for homework. Few children are so self-motivated that they will take care of their homework without any supervision, at least not in the early stages. However, resist the temptation to help too much. Homework is the student's responsibility, not the parent's.

The conventional wisdom says that the best place for a child to study is at a desk in his room. But I have talked to parents who have found that sitting around the family dining room table works better for them. The children do their homework while the parent does taxes or reads or works on another project. Mom or Dad are

there if the child needs help, but the time spent together is also important.

Some schools have established a homework hotline
the students can call for help when they've been absent or
don't remember what the assignment is. Some have
teachers on hand to explain the assignment if the student
gets stuck.

**If your child's teacher does not assign home-
work, devise some of your own.** I've found that some
parents want a page of written homework, something
where the child writes in the answers and the parent can
see that it is done. But the best homework might be
something different—reading a good book, memorizing
multiplication facts, writing in a journal, or playing a
math game.

If you're devising your own homework:

• Vary each evening's work. Short periods of study
each day work better than longer periods every other day
or once a week.

• Be careful not to go too fast. Children need a lot
of repetition and practice. If you go too fast, children
may do well for a time, and then become confused.

• Look over the educational games in the stores
near you. One of the laws of learning is that we learn better when we enjoy the process. Many companies have
capitalized on this by packaging geography, math, or
reading as games. Your child might like to spend part of
the homework time working alone, and part of it playing
an educational game.

Teach your child your moral values. Your children will meet people in school whose moral values dif-
fer from your own. Let your children know that they
should follow what they know to be right, that it's OK to
be different. Then, if at a later time, it is the "in" thing to

skip school or to experiment with drugs or to do something else that they know is wrong, they won't feel it's necessary to run with the pack.

Spend some time each day talking with your child. The easiest time is when you first meet your child after school or when you get home from work. Children are more likely to want to talk then. If you have established a routine, your child is more likely to open up and tell you when there are problems.

Recognize the signs that your child may be having problems at school. Children are often anxious during the first few days of school, just as we are the first few days on a new job. But if the problem persists or if your child feels sick in the mornings before school, there may be a deeper problem. Children don't verbalize very well. Sometimes they tell us in an indirect way. Watch for statements such as, "The teacher doesn't like me" or "It's so boring." Children who are doing well in school usually like it. Investigate if they don't. It may not be an academic problem. If your child is being intimidated by a bully or is having trouble making friends, he or she may be unhappy in school.

Encourage your child over the rough spots. Few of us, children included, are so multi-talented that we excel in everything. As adults, we can avoid the areas we don't like. Children don't have that option. Small wonder that they get discouraged! Let them know that you understand. Refuse to insist on "straight A's," even if your neighbor tells you that her child gets nothing else.

CHAPTER 5

When Children Lie

J ake's mother was distressed. "I know Jake is lying, but he's sticking to his story, and he won't back down," she said. "He has nothing to gain by it. Why does he lie?"

It happened on the day the school pictures were taken. When Jake walked into the kitchen after school, his mother asked him how school had gone. "Did you get your picture taken? Did you give your money to your teacher?" she asked.

"I gave the money to her, but she didn't want it. She just threw it into the garbage," said Jake.

Jake's mother was clearly frustrated when she came to see me. "Teachers don't do that," she said. "Why would he tell such a wild story?"

It's a good question. Why *do* children lie? Moreover, how do we teach them to tell the truth? Here are some suggestions:

Trust your child. Children do tell the truth most of the time. They are by nature very honest. So the first principle in teaching children to tell the truth is an obvious one: unless you know otherwise, assume he or she is telling the truth.

When, however, it is obvious that your child is lying, try to determine the reason for the lie. Children lie for the same reasons that adults do. Sometimes when we look at these reasons, the solution suggests itself.

Sometimes children lie to save face. They have done something they consider stupid and they would rather not admit it, so they tell a little "white" lie or they shade the truth a little bit. Or they tell a part of the story, skipping the embarrassing part.

"I was just standing there, doing nothing, and he hit me." (Never mind that Junior hit *him* this morning.)

In this case, getting the children together so you can hear both sides of the story may help. If the children know you are interested in helping them resolve their dispute, rather than finding someone to punish, they are more likely to tell the truth.

They may want to avoid getting into trouble. Children who are severely punished may find it easier to lie than to admit the offense.

"Who spilled the juice?" Mom asks, knowing full well that no one else has been in the kitchen but her 6-year-old son.

"I don't know," Johnny protests. "I don't know who did it."

Telling a lie may seem safer than getting a spanking for being so careless. Handing the child some paper towels so he can clean up the mess is often a better solution.

Kids may lie because they want something. The child who tells you "I'm the only one in the entire fifth grade who doesn't wear cowboy boots to school," probably suspects that you don't want to buy him a new pair of boots but figures that you couldn't bear to live with a deprived son on your hands. Two possibilities come to mind here. The first is to explain to him why he can't have cowboy boots. The second is to work out a plan to get the boots. He can either save or earn the money to pay for them, or he may choose to get boots the next time the family shops for shoes.

A lie helps them appear better than they think they are. We all want others to think we're OK. Children are no different. When they feel that they don't measure up, they may lie: "I had the best paper in the room, but I lost it." A lie like this is a sign that the child's self-esteem needs a boost. Helping your son do better in the area he is struggling with may solve the problem.

Another option is getting your child started in another field where he or she will do better. If, for example, your daughter has trouble with math, helping her with addition or multiplication facts may help. However, if math isn't "natural" for her, she may continue to feel inadequate. Helping her get started in a new hobby at which she can excel will enable her to feel—to know— that she is good at something, even when she struggles with something else. At any rate, your children should understand that you love them, even when they are having a hard time.

They may be caught up in the everyone-does-it snare. The child who says, "But Dad, all the other kids get to ———" (stay up as late as they want, watch whatever they want on television—fill in your own ending here) is not so different from the adult who says, "Everyone cheats a little on income taxes. Why should I pay more?" Setting a good example is important.

Sometimes children lie to get attention. A child at school says that he saw a burning house while his family was on vacation. So your child says that your family saw a forest fire on your summer trip. (It's better than admitting that you spent your vacation at home.) In this case, pointing out the difference between fact and make-believe may help. Or you might remind your son that the fire he saw was on television, and he will feel better if he corrects his misstatement.

Sometimes the child's perception is different from that of an adult. Children are not simply short adults. Their understanding is built on very limited experience. Remember my story of Jake and the money his mom had given him for the school photo? You can imagine his mother's surprise when I told her that Jake was telling the truth. I was surprised too, but then I hadn't looked at the event from Jake's perspective. This is what happened:

When Jake gave his money envelope to me, I told him to give it to the photographer's assistant when he went through the line. Jake did so. The assistant took the packet and tossed it into the nearby wastebasket. What Jake didn't realize was that she was using the wastebasket to collect the money. It made sense to me; she needed a large container. But to Jake, wastebaskets are filled with trash to be thrown away. (My husband, by the way, agrees with Jake, asserting that a conscientious janitor could easily wipe out the day's profits.)

EXPLAIN WHY TELLING
THE TRUTH IS IMPORTANT

We want to be believed. We want to be known as honest people. These reasons, obvious to adults, are not always so clear to a child. It's easier to teach truthfulness than it is to discourage lying; easier to reward than to punish—and much more effective. Here is a list of suggestions to encourage truthfulness.

Reward truth telling. Conversely, don't reward lying. This may seem to state the obvious, but we parents often reward actions we don't want, and punish those we do. When a child learns that lying pays, he or she may continue doing so, at least part of the time. Buying cowboy boots for your son when you suspect (know?) that many in fifth grade do *not* wear them, is not a good idea. It's better to suggest that your child ask directly for what he wants.

Build your child's self-esteem. Let your children know you love them just the way they are. This is true for all children, but it is especially true for the child whose achievements never quite measure up to those of a brother or sister. This child needs to know that your love and approval are always there; they are not dependent on accomplishments. The achiever also needs to know this. Otherwise he is under tremendous pressure to succeed at all costs, or to lie when he doesn't.

Set an example of honesty. Children want to be liked. They look to others for examples of acceptable behavior. They do what their parents do. If at your house "the check is in the mail" means "I'm looking for the money to pay for that," don't be too surprised to find that your child also fudges a little when it is convenient to do so.

Teach your child some polite but honest greetings. Some lies are socially acceptable, at least in some circles. Children usually do not see the difference; it is best to avoid them. In his book, *Hold on, Mr. President* Sam Donaldson tells the story of Miss Lillian, President Carter's mother. During his campaign for the presidency, President Carter had frequently told his audiences, "I'll never lie to you; I'll never mislead you." Pressed by a reporter about whether her son had ever told a lie, Miss Lillian confessed, "Well, maybe a white lie." Asked to define a white lie, she said, "Well, do you remember when you came in and I told you how pretty you look and how glad I was to see you?"

Teach your child some polite answers to questions that should not have been asked. Your child may not know how to comply with your instructions to keep certain information within the family without lying. For example, your neighbor asks your child how you're going to pay for your new car on your salary. Sometimes the best answer is "We don't talk about that" or "You'll have to ask my parents about that." You also can try to keep private family information from a young child so that he or she won't inadverently share it. But the best-laid plans don't always work.

Teach your child that it is preferable to remain silent rather than to lie. It may be difficult for you to accept this when you ask for information, especially if you fear your child has done something wrong. But forcing a child into a lie can start a cycle of lies and cover-ups until, even when he tells the truth, you find it hard to believe. Your child is more likely to tell the truth when he or she knows that your love and support will be there, even when he has done something wrong.

Teach your child to trust his own perceptions. Adults, after viewing a scene, often disagree about what they saw or about what happened. Children seldom do. Children are so eager to please that they will agree with whatever the first speaker says, provided that the questioner accepts it and the child is not being blamed. What the first child says happened will probably be readily agreed to by the rest of the group. This isn't lying. The child just assumes that what he saw can't be right, since it's not what others saw. Teachers who want to get to the bottom of things have learned to interview young children one at a time.

I did my student teaching in a laboratory school. As student teachers, we worked in a classroom in the morning and went to classes in the afternoon. In the hour following the morning session, we were to escort the students outside the building, see each student off, and clean up the classroom. We also had to eat lunch and drive across town in time for our afternoon class. We were always in a hurry.

One day a first grader wasn't picked up with the others. For 40 minutes we tried to appear more patient than we felt, while the child fought back tears and told us something had happened to her daddy; he was never late. He never had been late before, so we kept assuring her that he would be here "right away."

When a car approached the driveway, one of our group said, "Here he is!"

The girl got into the car, and the car drove off. Before we got back inside the building, another car drove up. One of the student teachers recognized the child's father.

A month earlier a primary child in another city had been kidnapped from a school. We were all aware of it, and so were all the parents. They were terrified by it. So now we had to try to explain to the father just who it was who had picked up his child. All of us had been standing within two feet of the car. One teacher had even opened the car door. The six of us agreed on three points:

1. It was a sedan.

2. The car was light colored. (Some said it was green; some said blue.)

3. It was driven by a man. (Some said he was young; some didn't know.)

No one had looked at the license plates. We didn't agree on the make of the car. . . . You get the picture.

The story does have a happy ending. The mother, re-

alizing that her child would think she had been aban-
doned forever when the father was detained in class, had
asked her brother to pick her up. Which he did.

You understand my point. If adults find it difficult to
state the facts, it should not be surprising to find that
children's stories sometimes get muddled. Learning to
observe and relate what one sees takes time and practice.
Children need help with this.

We parents want what is best for our children.
Wishing to spare them the pain of childhood mistakes,
we may find it hard to tolerate lying. But growing up
does involve mistakes and suffering the consequences of
those mistakes. So you may find that your child is less
truthful than you would hope as he or she progresses
toward maturity. But if you encourage truthfulness and
are consistent in your example of honesty, you can expect
your child to accept your values and to tell the truth, even
when it is hard to do so.

CHAPTER 6

Getting Along With Others

It was just an ordinary fight, as fights go. No one started it, and both boys were just standing there when the other one punched him. At least that's the way they told it to me.

It all started innocently enough. The day was hot, and the cafeteria line was long. Roy leaned against the wall while he waited. When the line moved, he lost his place. So he moved back into line. Tom, also in line, thought he was cutting in. In the noise of the cafeteria Roy didn't hear Tom's objections, so Tom pushed him out of line. That's when the fists began to fly.

By the time the cook waded in, there were forks and mashed potatoes and spicy applesauce flying everywhere. And the cook wanted to know why I didn't teach my students how to behave in the cafeteria. So there went my lunch period.

I suspected the cause of the fight as soon as they told me about it. Tom, whose speech was hard to understand, often showed people what he meant. He told Roy where his place was, and when Roy didn't go there, he tried to push him back in his place. Roy, who had a hearing loss, didn't hear Tom and thought he was pushing for no reason.

I wish that all disagreements were so easily settled. Once the boys heard the other side of the story, they were glad to find a kindred spirit. Our cook was a good sport too. She accepted their apologies and their offer to make amends by wiping tables.

You don't have to watch the evening news very long to know that people (and nations) often quarrel and fight, and that children don't simply outgrow this by the time they become adults. While disagreements are common, learning to resolve them takes some work, and this is a place where children usually can use some help. Fortunately, families are the ideal place for people to learn how to get along with each other.

Children are quick to use the same methods for resolving conflicts that they see others around them using. If you and your spouse enjoy a good rousing argument now and then, you probably aren't surprised when your children roar at each other and at their friends when they disagree. And an abusive parent often finds that an abused child is abusing another child.

Children also learn to resolve conflicts by watching how their parents discipline them. When parents talk over disputes, children learn to work out solutions. Parents who spank, on the other hand, are teaching their children that we hit other people when we disagree with them.

Few children (or adults for that matter) are so reasonable that they can always discuss a situation calmly. When tempers flare, it may be necessary to declare a time-out before talking over the problem. If talking is not

enough, try to work out a plan so that when disagreements come up the children know what to do. A workable plan might be: "Susan must ask before she borrows
my sweater, and I may choose to say no, if I want to." Or,
"When I want to play with Tom's truck, I'll ask if I may
trade one of my toys for a while."

Sometimes, when children fight, argue, or bicker,
they aren't really disagreeing. They are playing their favorite game of "Let's bug our parents." Children want attention. Even negative attention is better than no
attention. I stumbled on a good plan of action for this
one day at school.

Two fourth-grade boys were really slugging it out, so
I stopped them. I was going to talk things over with them,
but there was another incident across the playground, so
I told them where to sit until I got back. I was careful to
seat them far enough apart so they wouldn't start the fight
again. From across the playground I could see that they
were edging closer. By the time I was ready to start back,
they were sitting together and talking, so I decided to wait
a while. When it looked as if things were friendly, I
walked over and said, "Well, what did you decide?" It was
plain to see that they were friends by this time.

I have found that younger children may need help
with this. It helps to ask them to sit with me while I ask
first one child, and then the other, to tell what happened,
and how they feel about it. I have needed to point out
that responses such as "So?" or "I'm going to get you as
soon as we get outside!" aren't helpful, so the child has to
respond in some other way.

This technique has been especially useful in dealing
with the-boys-are-chasing-us complaint that teachers
often get from girls on the playground. The girls could
easily stop the action themselves by refusing to run, but

it's nice to get the teacher's attention, so they complain. The boys usual response is, "I thought we were playing."

In the family it helps to hold a family council to draw up some family rules. It's better to have everyone discuss and agree on the rules, but if no agreement can be reached, parents may need to simply announce what the rules are. Be sure the list includes the areas in which your children are most likely to disagree. Your list might also include such items as these:

• Family members may go into another's room only after knocking and receiving permission. (Decide beforehand how the rules will apply to parents.)

• Name calling and put-downs are not allowed.

• Hurting anyone physically is not allowed. (Be as specific here as you need to be.)

• Toys, clothes, and other property can be borrowed only with permission from the owner.

When you have decided on a list of rules, set a time to review them to determine which ones are working and which need to be revised or dropped.

So far I have been talking about the ordinary disagreements that crop up in any family, the stresses of everyday living. Sometimes disputes aren't so simple. Children who live under undue stress will probably squabble more among themselves. If the stress is temporary, say a holiday, or the visit of relatives, things will probably settle down by themselves when the event is over.

If the stressful event is likely to continue, as for example, when an ailing grandparent moves into the child's room, or when a family member is seriously ill, the child may need an outlet. Friends who invite the child over from time to time may relieve the stress. Enrolling the child in an outside activity or club may help.

Sometimes, though, a child fights, bickers, or argues,

even when there is no disagreement to be resolved. Sometimes a child just doesn't get along with others. Some, in fact, seem to enjoy picking on others. If this behavior persists, the family will want to seek the help of a family counselor. Your child's school may offer counseling services or may be able to recommend some therapists. Shop around until you find one who suits your family, and check to see whether your health insurance will pay at least part of the cost. Be aware that many counselors who work with children will want to work with the entire family, at least part of the time. The family dynamics will change if the behavior of one member changes.

There are pitfalls to avoid when helping children learn to get along with one another. Among them are:

Requiring older children to always give in to the younger child because he is little. This is not only unfair to the older child, it is harmful to the younger child as well. This younger child is learning that everyone should give in to him. Entering a school situation where he or she is expected to take turns can be a painful experience.

Requiring them to always settle their own problems. While the purpose of discipline is to teach children to manage their own behavior, this tactic may be allowing a strong-willed child to dominate a more passive one. That isn't good for either one.

Showing favoritism to one child over another. This often keeps children fighting for the Mom/Dad-likes-me-best position.

Following these guidelines will not produce a Christmas card family in your home, where everyone smiles lovingly at all times. Nevertheless, children should be able to live together without tearing each other apart. Verbally or physically.

CHAPTER 7

Your Child's Friends

Have you ever been caught in a dilemma, torn between knowing that children must choose their own friends and the fear that poor choices will lead to friends that undermine your teaching and lead to bad behavior? If so, you've probably already learned that when you object to the behavior of your childrens' friends, it may make them defend their friends all the more, clinging to friendships that might otherwise be given up. Here are some suggestions for helping your child choose the right friends.

Be sure your child knows what acceptable behavior is. Set an example of the standards you want your child to follow. If, for example, you do not want your child to use four-letter words, *never* watch those television programs where actors use these words.

Teach your child the social skills necessary for making and keeping friends. Teach Mary to take turns and to share. Provide Johnny with toys and equipment that he can share with others.

Make your home the gathering place for your children and their friends. This may mean that the new Chippendale has to wait until the children are older. The worn spots in your lawn may make your home less the showplace you had hoped it might be. But you will know your child's friends, and you can set the standards for behavior, at least up to a point. That's very important. As one father pointed out, "I'm not raising grass; I'm raising boys."

Volunteer as a room parent, or helper, at your child's school. School is the place where many friendships are made. Get to know your child's friends.

Get to know the parents of your child's friends. While you can't always tell what a child is like by meeting his or her parents, meeting the parents will help you understand their child. You may meet some obnoxious parents with charming children, or you may meet some lovely parents with children you hope to never see again. Knowing this can help you set limits if you need to.

Take your child to church groups. While no church pretends that its young members are perfect, most of them have parents with common goals, and the activities are planned with character building in mind.

Foster your child's self-confidence. Children who feel good about themselves are usually not so fearful of making new friends that they hang on to those they dislike. A self-confident child is also more likely to stand up to friends when they are planning to do something he or she knows is wrong.

If your child's friends will not comply with your standards, you may need to send the friends home. This is, of course, much more easily done when you are dealing with younger children. Forbidding an older child to see a friend may not work if the child can meet that friend somewhere else. In this case, a change of scenery may help. Summer camp or a vacation may introduce new friends who will replace the one in question.

Let me give an example from my own childhood:

My siblings and I sat on the porch and moped.

"You must go home now," my mother had told Clayton. "We don't use words like that here."

And so he'd left. We watched him walk down the road, his hands were in his pockets, his shoulders drooped. "Now we won't have anyone to play with," we whined.

Mother was unmoved by our protests. "You can play by yourselves," she said.

Still we argued. "He was just showing off. We would never use those words, even if we heard Clayton using them."

"You are not allowed to talk like that. And neither are your friends while they are here," she had said, before turning back to her work. (Mothers of four children always seem to be able to find something that needs doing.)

As it turned out, my mother knew more about human nature than we did. With four children in the family, we always had someone to play with. Clayton, an only child, had no one. We had barely gotten down to pouting in earnest when we spotted Clayton walking back up the road. He walked past the pouty group on the front porch and straight to my mother. His apology was straightforward and sincere. And soon we were happily playing together again.

Many parents of an only child worry about their child making friends. "How can he or she learn to share and take turns," they wonder, "when there is no one in the family to share with?" I've discovered that the parents of only children are so aware of the possible problem that they take care to prevent it. They invite other children over to play at their house. They enroll their child in a play group. They take their child to places where he meets other children.

The child most in need of extra help, in my experience, has been the youngest child in a large family. This child may be used to older brothers and sisters giving in or doing things for him or her. Kevin was one such child.

He came to school expecting everyone to always let him be first and to give in any time he wanted something. When I explained that he would have to take turns with the others, he said, "But I'm just little."

"Everyone here is just little," I pointed out.

"But I'm only 5," he insisted.

"Everyone here is only 5," I replied.

It was painful for him to adjust to a situation where he was no longer the only small child and had to take turns and share.

Friends are important. They teach children how to evaluate people. They help children understand who they are. They help to socialize the child. They teach him how to get along with others. They can reinforce the things you teach at home. And they make life more fun. It's important for your child to have friends, but he or she must learn to choose the right friends.

CHAPTER 8

The Shy Child

I rummaged through the remnants of my high school Spanish, trying to find the words to tell this tiny child that things would get better, that someday soon she would like kindergarten. Dropped off at the door by an older sister in a hurry to get to her own classroom, Maria was clearly frightened. I doubted that she knew enough English to understand what was going on around her, and the other children barely noticed this brave little girl who was trying to mask the tears that dripped off her chin.

Sometimes shyness hurts. Many children feel shy about a new situation. Teachers see very few aggressive children on the first day of school. (Don't even think of asking about the second day!) For children who are temporarily shy, the solution is fairly simple.

You and I understand the child's feelings. We've felt the same way when facing a new boss or visiting an oral surgeon. We understand their fears, and so we do for them what we would like to have done for us when we are frightened. We drive the child to school on the first day; we walk the child to the classroom and meet the new teacher. For self-confident children this seems to work pretty well.

But what about Maria and the children like her, children who are so painfully shy that meeting new people is painful; children who are terrified by occasions that should be fun?

Fortunately, many shy children have at least one parent who was also shy as a child. If you are such a person, sharing experiences about how you overcame your shyness may help your child. Also share some of the silly things you did to escape social situations.

I once had a teacher who told of agonizing over a speech she had to give when she was in junior high. Painfully shy, she thought she would never live through the experience. The speech went very well, she said, until she was leaving the stage. That's when she noticed she was wearing her dress inside out.

She laughed when she told about it. "After that," she said, "speeches were easier. I figured I could never do any worse than that."

If you, on the other hand, are one of those outgoing people who loves meeting and talking to people, you must accept the fact that your child's pain is real. Telling him or her to brace up and be more like a friend or a brother who is never afraid will probably make things worse. Listening and making comments such as, "That must have been very hard for you" or "I'm glad you tried," may help more.

Here are some other suggestions which may make life easier for your shy child:

Talk with your child. It helps shy children to understand that people like them just the way they are. I have found shy children to be very sensitive to the feelings of others. Some of the children who have been the most sympathetic and helpful to other shy newcomers have themselves been shy and afraid when they started school. There is nothing wrong with feeling shy.

Prompt your child, when necessary, but refuse to talk for him or her. If, for example, your child doesn't answer when someone asks his name, you might ask, "Can you say, 'My name is David?'" If your child still says nothing, let it go at that. Don't allow a child to use his shyness to manipulate others. For instance, allowing an older brother or sister to speak for him or to take care of him in social situations is not good.

Enroll the shy child in his or her own activities. The children may all go to swimming lessons, for example, but to different classes.

Never apologize for your child's shyness. Even an innocent statement such as "She's shy" may teach a child that such behavior is expected.

Look around for another quiet or shy child whom you might invite to play with your child. A shy child is less likely to be overwhelmed by another shy child. A smaller play group may also help. Groups of two or three are less threatening than larger groups.

Help your child do well in something. If he or she can do well in a hobby, music lessons, or sports, your child is more likely to feel good about himself/herself. Don't insist, however, that your child perform in public until he feels comfortable about doing so. That first public performance must be successful.

Look for jobs or chores that expose your child to people. Jobs, such as taking up tickets at a school game or passing out the dessert at a party, require social mingling without much talking. One of my favorite jobs when I was in school was working as a cashier in the school cafeteria. I met everyone without thinking about what I would say.

Enlist the help of your child's teachers. Handing out papers, erasing chalkboards, watering plants, or other school chores can help a shy child feel part of the group. Teaming the shy child with another student to work together on a project may also help.

Practice social courtesies with your child. Knowing how to order food in a restaurant, how to make introductions, or how to pay in a store will make your child more comfortable in social situations.

Compliment your child when he does well. Ignore social blunders, if at all possible. Never correct a shy child in public.

Be careful not to let your shy child become too dependent on you. It's important to let the shy child know that he can handle the situation. If you take your child to school, for example, be sure that he or she knows you will leave. If the child is upset, tell him or her that you will be there as soon as school is over. Staying too long tells the child that there might be something to be afraid of and prolongs or delays the parting.

Following these suggestions will not turn your shy child into the life of the party, nor would you want to do so. Still, a child need not be so shy that meeting and playing with others is painful, especially when a little help from you can make a difference.

CHAPTER 9

The Picky Eater

I was having lunch with my favorite fifth grader. It seemed to be the right time to talk about good food choices. She listened patiently, then said, "Don't worry about me, Grandma. I know all about the four food groups." And then she added, "It's just that all the things I like are in the fifth food group—junk food."

It's not just grandmas who worry about children's eating habits. Many parents do too. Usually it's because the child doesn't want to eat at mealtimes, doesn't eat enough, or prefers the wrong foods. Here are some suggestions to help your picky eater:

Make mealtime a happy time. Save the discussions of poor report cards, family finances, and poor table manners for another time.

Serve only nourishing food. Have dessert only once a week or serve fruit for dessert.

Stock up on healthful snacks. Throw out those snack foods that are heavy in fats, salt, or sugar.

Substitute nutritious food your child likes for those he dislikes. Many children dislike vegetables. There may be a good reason for this. Alexandra Logue, from the University of New York, states: "Some children are genetically sensitive to certain tastes. They especially find vegetables to be more bitter." Many vegetables have similar nutritional value. Your child may be willing to eat peas, for example, but refuses to eat spinach.

Try a different form of the food your child dislikes. A child who disdains cooked carrots may like raw carrot sticks. Many children dislike casseroles but may like the same ingredients unmixed.

Experiment with flavorings that improve or change the taste of food. A school cook confided that she adds vanilla to orange juice. It makes the juice taste sweeter without adding sugar. A parent says her daughter won't eat string beans unless she sprinkles them with chicken-style seasoning. Another parent adds vanilla and raisins to the morning oatmeal.

Present the food in a colorful manner. Your child might like to make open-faced sandwiches or salads with faces. Use bread, spread with peanut butter; or use a peach or pear half for the base of a salad. Add raisins or cereal for the eyes, nose, and mouth, and a thatch of coconut for hair.

Look at your schedule. If your child fills up on snacks after school and has little appetite for the evening meal, consider changing the dinner hour. If breakfast is a problem, consider getting your child up early enough for a brief playtime before breakfast.

Teach your child why we eat nutritious food. Your children are rapidly moving toward the time when they will make their own food choices. The granddaughter I mentioned earlier in this chapter launched herself into a nutritional food program when her softball coach convinced the team that they could play better if they ate right.

Don't let your child get into the habit of skipping meals and then asking for something to eat soon after. You might require such a child to stay at the table until everyone is finished, and allow no snacks until the next meal. (Very young children, however, may need something to eat before they go to bed.)

Avoid power struggles about eating. You don't want to turn today's finicky eater into tomorrow's eating disorder. Be patient. A growth spurt may change your picky eater into a chowhound tomorrow.

Keep in mind that a child's stomach is very small. What seems like a small amount to an adult may be enough for a child. Children who are being regularly checked by a doctor, and who are making adequate weight gains, are probably eating enough. Requiring a child to clean up his plate may encourage the child to eat too much, putting on fat that may be hard to take off later.

Breakfast is especially important. If your child doesn't like traditional breakfast foods, substitute favorite foods—sandwiches instead of cereal, for instance.

Keep in mind that picky eaters are found only in families where there is an abundance of food and choices about what is eaten. I once worked in a school in a low-income neighborhood. The students ate lunch, family style, in the classrooms. One day an 8-year-old picked up a serving bowl, now empty of the green beans it had held, and began licking it. Glancing sideways at me, she said, "I know this is bad manners, but it tastes so-o-o good!" Thinking of my own picky eaters at home, I decided that sometimes licking the bowl is OK.

CHAPTER 10

Teaching Responsibility

In some ways, being responsible is the same as being dependable, but it's also more than that. There are some people I can depend on to always be late, but that's not the same as being responsible. I like the definition of responsibility I found in my Webster's dictionary. Responsibility means: "Being able to account for one's own behavior, taking on the duties and obligations appropriate for one's age, and not blaming others when things go wrong."

We've all met the person who's never to blame for anything. When he's 4 he says, "My mother didn't tell me not to get my shoes wet." At 9 he's saying, "Well, nobody told me to come in and do my homework." At 17 he's saying, "I wouldn't have been driving that fast if you hadn't said I had to be in by midnight." At 30 he says, "I would be able to keep a job if my dad had played ball with me when I was little." At 50 he says, "I'm overweight because my mother made me clean up my plate when I was a child." This person never admits responsibility for his own actions. It's always someone else's fault.

It's easier to teach responsibility when the child is very young, but it's never too late to begin. It's harder—and it takes longer—to break a habit than it does to stop one from getting started.

The most important thing to remember in teaching responsibility is to never do for the child what the child can do for himself or herself. Here are some suggestions:

Encourage children to dress themselves. When a young baby reaches out his arms to help you put on his shirt, encourage him or her. When the child is older, let him choose his own clothes, within the limits you have set. Let him get himself ready, helping only when he needs help. Most parents do this naturally; they don't even think about it. But some parents will continue to do things for their child long after the child is capable.

I once had a first grade student throw a temper tantrum because I wouldn't put his coat on for him. So I said, "Why don't you just carry it along to the playground?" He learned how to put his coat on as soon as he discovered how cold it was outside.

There are times, though, when you may need to enlist the aid of others. It often takes less time to do the job ourselves rather than teach a child to do it, or to wait for him to get it done. Big sisters are especially willing to take care of younger children. And children are quite willing to get help from anyone willing to give it. They like service.

I've used the illustration of dressing a child. I should point out that some coats and boots are next to impossible for a child to fasten. When a child really can't do something, he should be helped.

Teach your children to get themselves up in the

morning and get ready for school. Buy an alarm clock and teach them to set it and turn it off. Later, they'll be able to have themselves ready for school on time without any reminders from you. Some children like this and never need to be reminded, but check to make sure.

Don't accept the blame when your child doesn't follow through. Notes to the teacher explaining that you overslept, or that it's your fault that the homework didn't get done, or that his bad behavior in class is because of some incident at home give the kind of excuses that your child doesn't need. He *is* responsible for his behavior. Let him accept it.

Don't accept the consequences for your child's actions. One mother said that when her son was forbidden to ride the school bus because of his rowdy behavior, she drove him to and from school. In telling the story she lamented that if she had it to do over again he would walk the two miles. She would follow in the car if it was too dark to be safe, but he would walk. Unfortunately, her son was in serious trouble with the law by the time she learned this.

Be responsible yourself. If you are always on time, your child knows that's important. If you take care of your bills, your child will also likely do so.

Household chores teach children to be responsible. Begin with small things—helping to fold and put away the towels, for example—and then go on to larger tasks, such as cleaning their room or mowing the lawn. Be sure that each child has his or her own jobs. If you ask, for example, that the children clean a room they share, one child may do most or all of the work while the other watches or supervises.

Some children aren't very good at following multi-step directions. Sometimes it helps to have a written list so they can cross off the items when they are done. It also helps if the directions are broken down into shorter steps. Instead of "clean up your room," the list might be:

1. Put your toys in your toybox.
2. Put clean sheets on your bed.
3. Put your dirty clothes in your hamper.
4. Shake your throw rug.

The list can be as long as it needs to be, but if it is very long, you probably need to break it into shorter segments with a break in between. Item 5 on the list might be, for example, "Go outside and play for 15 minutes."

Caring for a pet can teach responsibility. Be sure to choose a pet that is sturdy enough to be suitable. Easter chicks, for example, are cute, but they are too fragile a pet for a young child. Choosing a puppy for a child can be tricky too. Be sure your child is old enough to care for one. Choose a breed that is suitable for a young child. Our son was brokenhearted when he had to give up a dog he had loved and trained, because as an adult, the dog grew vicious. Choosing carefully can avoid that.

CHAPTER 11

Money Matters

When I was a child I asked my mother for an allowance. I had my weekly budget planned. Every day on the way home from school I'd stop at the store to buy penny candy. My mother didn't think much of a budget spent only on candy. She explained why candy every day wasn't good for me, adding that spending money only for candy wasn't a wise use of money. At the time I wasn't convinced. Now, as an adult, I am glad she didn't give me an allowance with no restrictions on how I spent it.

Children who spend their allowances solely on personal wishes or on impulse buying often grow into adults who find themselves in serious financial trouble, because they use their credit cards in the same way. While it's possible to learn to manage money as an adult, it is much easier and less painful to learn as a child.

So how do we teach our children to use money responsibly? Every family is different; what works in one family may not work in another. Still, some ideas are worth considering:

Begin early. Learning to spend money wisely is a long-term project. Some skills, especially those involving math, may have to wait until the child has the skill necessary to cope. But with some parental help, even very young children can take part.

Look at your own family spending. Your children look to you as an example of how things should be done. When they see you budgeting your income to include necessary expenses, giving to church and charities, and making deposits to savings accounts before spending on extras, they see an example of how to manage their own resources. If, on the other hand, your family spends freely at the beginning of each paycheck and goes without necessities or dodges creditors at the end of the pay period, the children may have problems in managing their own money.

A child's allowance should be large enough for him or her to plan and manage a budget. Whether your child's allowance is given as wages for work performed or as a part of the family budget, it should be large enough to include spending, giving, and saving. An allowance that enables a child to spend freely on impulse is simply a handout. This does not encourage good spending habits.

Be flexible. Adjust the allowance, if you need to, but resist the temptation to rescue your child everytime he overspends. He will not be learning financial responsibility if he can borrow every time he "must" have something. On the other hand, emergencies do come up. Perhaps your child's budget does not allow for the proper clothing to wear to an important event. You may need to help out.

Allow your child to make mistakes. Be slow to offer advice based on personal preference, and even slower to say, "I told you so." We all learn from our mistakes if we are allowed to do so, and learning from mistakes is easier if we don't have to defend them.

Teach your child to give. Money is not something to hoard or to use as power over people who have less. Your child will learn to empathize with others as he learns to share with others.

Teach your child to save for things. Piggy banks are helpful, but children should see saving as a way to get something they want, not as an end in itself. This idea makes saving easier for a child. It also teaches a child to work toward a goal.

Teach your child to spend wisely. The children I have taught in school learned how to count money very early. But they had very little idea of what that amount of money would buy. Here is a list of projects designed to teach children to spend wisely. The list is by no means conclusive. You'll want to adapt these ideas to suit the ages of your children or devise some new projects of your own.

● Allow your child to choose and pay for his or her own clothing. (A younger child will need some help with this.) The child might begin by choosing school clothing within the limits you set, before going on to choosing and paying for the entire wardrobe. Encourage the child to assess his or her present wardrobe and develop a plan before shopping for more clothing.

● Loan your calculator to your child to take along while you shop for groceries. Have your child tally the price of each item as you put it into the shopping cart. Ask for the total price before you check out.

● Have your child plan and give a birthday party for a member of the family. Have him compare the price of a cake that he can make at home with the price of a cake purchased at the store. Have him compare the cost of napkins, cups, and paper plates at different stores.

• Have your child plan a dinner for the family at a restaurant. The child can call restaurants to find one he or she likes, one whose prices are within the family budget. He or she can make the reservations, leave a tip, and pay for the bill.

• Have your child compare the price of raw potatoes with that of a packaged potato product, such as scalloped potatoes or potato chips.

• Have your child compare the price of raw apples with the cost of applesauce or apple juice.

• Let your child buy a package of his or her favorite junk food and calculate the cost of a pound of the product. Compare this with that of some nutritional food product that your child likes.

• Compare the cost of a water-based beverage (like a fruit-flavored drink) with the cost of water from your kitchen faucet.

For most of us, the way to make the most of our income is to make the best use of what we have. Increasing our income substantially is usually not possible. Managing what they have is an important skill for children to learn. This is not a skill which can be learned overnight. Expect to spend some time working at it. (Most adults are still learning, or need to.) Expect some mistakes along the way, but don't be discouraged by them. Hopefully, with time and patience on your part, your child will learn to handle money wisely.

CHAPTER 12

About Racial Differences

What color is the rest of you?"

An interesting question, one worth the interruption of the story I was reading to my kindergarten class. "What do you mean?" I asked.

"Well," said this 5-year old, "your face and hands are white, but your legs are black. Are you White or are you Black? What color is the rest of you?"

I hadn't thought how my long sleeves and dark stockings might make the color of my skin doubtful to a child of another race. Children do notice racial differences. True, they don't think these differences matter all that much—not unless we teach them otherwise. If you want your children to do well in a world made up of differing cultures, races, and classes, here are some ways of doing this:

Your child is more likely to meet and like people whose background differs from his or her own if you yourself do so on a regular basis. Join a church or other organization that includes members of other races and cultures.

Encourage your child to include friends of other races and cultures when planning birthday parties or other events. Invite them to play in your yard. Take them along on family picnics.

Examine your own prejudices. If you wish no ill to others but believe that people from other races, cultural groups, or economic classes belong "in their place," your child may think that "their place" is an inferior one.

Steer clear of ethnic jokes, slang terms, and dialect jokes. These types of references to racial or cultural groups are offensive. Avoid them.

Stereotypes, even those we may think are flattering, may be resented. An Asian woman once told me how much it offended her to be continually told how bright Asian students are.

"We are all individuals," she said. "Some of us are bright. Some of us struggle—just like everybody else."

Call members of a group by the name they wish to be called. Be aware, however, that many consider themselves to be American or Canadian and would rather not be identified with any subculture. When my friend Linda is asked whether she wants to be called Black or African American, she answers with, "Call me Linda."

Enlist the help of a friend, minister, or teacher from a culture different than your own. Many will be glad to help your child understand what it is like to belong to another race or culture.

DEALING WITH PREJUDICE

If, in spite of your best efforts, your child shows evidence of prejudice, first examine the level of your child's feelings. I once rescued an African American kindergarten student from a group of Caucasian youngsters who were trying to wash the dark color off his skin. (He didn't particularly want to be rescued; he was scrubbing away too.) Dealing with this problem didn't take more than a discussion of what causes differences in skin color.

At a deeper level, a child who has just been punched in the nose may respond by saying, "I hate all ———." In this case you need to explain that while anger at this particular person may be justified, carrying that anger to everyone who is a member of that race or culture is not appropriate. You also might want to keep an eye on the attitudes of your child's friends. If they're not setting a good example, involving your child in a supervised activity, such as Scouts or 4H, may help.

Finally, you need to take it seriously if your child joins a group that vandalizes churches or synagogues, paints hate slogans, or burns crosses. Your child needs to understand that such actions are not only wrong, they are against the law. I'd recommend professional counseling in such cases.

Remember, prejudice can be very subtle. If I say that I love everyone but am indifferent to their needs, I am prejudiced. If I accept their friendship only because they are like me, I am biased. For the opposite of love is not hate. It is indifference.

CHAPTER 13

Tactics for Tantrums

I saw my first temper tantrum during my first year of teaching. I was 20 years old, trying to look older and more professional than I knew I was. I knew something was up when the principal sent for me right before school. Teachers need to be at their doors when the students are coming in.

I heard the noise before I got there. Charlie, my fourth grader, was lying on the floor outside the principal's office, kicking and screaming. A crowd had gathered to watch, including the principal and Charlie's mother.

The principal saw me coming. "Your student?" she asked.

I nodded.

"Take charge!" she ordered.

I come from an old German family. In old German families children do not lie on the floor and kick and scream. I had never seen anything like this. So I did the only thing I could think of. "Come on, Charlie," I said. "Let's go back to our room."

The screaming stopped. Charlie stood up and walked calmly with me to our classroom. I was too surprised to look back.

Tantrums are not something a child will just naturally outgrow without help. A girl who gets what she wants by kicking and screaming will likely move on to raging at her parents when she is a teenager, and then abuse her own children when she is an adult.

Sometimes the tantrums are so violent that the child hurts himself or herself. One mother told me that her child broke her tooth off by banging her head against the sink during a tantrum. And I once had an eighth grade student ram her arm through a hall window as she raged at another student. Her cuts required stitches.

Here are some guidelines to follow if your child has tantrums:

Keep in mind that your goal is to teach your child to handle anger or frustration in a socially acceptable way. This means that you will not cave in to your child's demands just because he is embarrassing you in public. It also means you will refuse to be drawn into any of the quick fixes recommended by well-meaning friends or relatives.

Be very controlled when dealing with a tantrum. If you lose your temper or resort to any action that suggests you are out of control, your child is likely to become frightened, and the situation will become worse. Think of yourself driving a car that's skidding on icy pavement. It's much more scary if the car coming toward you is also out of control.

When your child is having the tantrum:

• Isolate him or her as much as possible. If you are at home or in a safe place, walk to another room where you are out of sight but are still able to make sure that the child is not hurting himself or herself or trashing the area. If you are in a public place, move farther away and act busy with something else. Most tantrums are a public performance; if the audience moves away, the tantrum stops. If this one does not, it may be necessary to pick the child up and carry him or her to your car or to his room. If the child is too big to carry, you may need to wait until he or she calms before proceeding further.

- If you touch the child, be as gentle as possible. Caressing and stroking may soothe a baby; an older child may be provoked further by any touching.

- Be very careful in using your voice. Children respond more to the tone of voice than they do to the actual words. A baby may be calmed by your singing or speaking softly. An older child may not be.

- Keep in mind that some children aren't nearly as out of control as they seem. Simply telling your child to "cut it out" may work.

AFTER THE TANTRUM IS OVER:

- Give the child some time to collect himself or herself. Depending on the child's age, he or she may be upset enough to need at least an hour before being calm enough to discuss the incident with you. You might say, "You may spend some time in your room, playing quietly, and then we will discuss what has happened."

- Plan together what action you and the child will take the next time he feels he will be out of control. Begin the discussion by stating clearly what the child did. You might say, "When I didn't buy the toy you wanted, you stomped and screamed at me. I had to carry you to the car. That kind of behavior is unacceptable."

At this point most children will probably respond, "I won't ever do that again."

Accept the apology but realize that this is not a plan.

What you are working for is a socially acceptable way for your child to act when he or she is angry. So you might say, "Before we go to the store next time, we will make a list of the things we will buy. If you see something you want, you may ask for it, but we will not buy anything that is not on the list until we have talked about it at home and decided whether or not to buy it."

Another possible plan might be to say, "If you feel you are going to be out of control, you may hold my hand. You will tell me what is bothering you, and I will listen. We will decide together what we will do."

An alternative for the child who will not plan is to say, "Why don't we think about this for a while and see what we can come up with." But don't take the child to the store (or wherever the tantrum occurred) until you can come up with a workable plan.

In school the problem often occurs on the playground. If the child will not agree to a plan (usually because he says the tantrum was not his fault), I then tell the child that he may not go to the playground until he can come up with a plan. I have never had a student miss more than one recess.

• Refuse to cave in to any plan which causes you to give in to the child's demands. If you give in to what the child wants, he or she learns to have a tantrum when he or she wants something. You don't want that. The plan must be acceptable to both of you.

• Be sure to have your child checked by a doctor. One mother told me how her 3-year-old would throw herself on the floor and thrash around. Her pediatrician helped her understand how to deal with tantrums, and she was working on it. One morning her daughter was watching cartoons on television while her mother washed dishes in the kitchen. When the mother glanced into the living room, she saw her daughter rolling and kicking on the floor. Realizing that children do not have tantrums when they are by themselves, the mother took her back to see the doctor. A brain scan determined that the child was having seizures.

• Look for other possible causes for the tantrums. Remember Charlie? He had asthma and sometimes missed school. After an absence he sometimes didn't want to come back to school. He had learned over the years that his tantrums embarrassed his mother, and she would keep him home rather than face his tantrums in public. He gave them up when he learned that they no longer worked.

• Look at the area where your child has tantrums. It helps to plan in advance. If, for example, your child often has a tantrum when it is time to leave the park, announce in advance, "You may play for an hour. I will tell you when you have five minutes more to play. Then we will leave." If he or she will not abide by this, announce that you will not come back to the park until he or she is willing to stick to the plan.

• Look at your own ways of handling anger and frustration. Are you calm and controlled? Or is your behavior a model for your child's own tantrums? Remember that your child loves you, wants to be like you, sees the world's ideal adult in you. (Scary, isn't it?)

• Look at the time of your child's tantrums. Do they come when your child is tired? If so, more rest may be needed. Noise or confusion seems to agitate some children. If this is a problem, you may need to schedule more "quiet" time, time when the child can play or read without outside stimulation. Some parents have found that quiet, soothing music also helps.

If your child is lashing out at other people, you may want to look into putting him or her into a smaller, more organized play or school group. Another possibility would be to place the child with older or with younger children, where he or she is on a socially equal status with the others.

• Look to see whether you or someone else is provoking the tantrums. Tickling, teasing, or bullying may be more than your child can handle.

IF THE TANTRUMS PERSIST:

If you have tried these suggestions and your child is still unable to handle his frustration or anger, or if your child is hurting himself or is striking out at other people or at animals, you need to take him to see a counselor.

Keep in mind that many counselors will want to work with the whole family, not just the child with the problem. Some parents resist this. "The family isn't the problem," they say. "It's just this one child who has the problem."

While this may be perfectly true, the child is acting in a family setting. If the behavior of one person changes, the family dynamics change too. When your "family terror" begins to shape up, he or she may threaten the position of your "perfect child," and that child may try to push the "terror" back into position.

CHAPTER 14

Stealing

I worried about this newcomer to my classroom. He couldn't know that his background presented a textbook example of a troubled child. Nathan had grown up seeing his mother abused by a series of boyfriends. She often left him alone to care for his twin brothers. He was 5 years old when social workers stepped in to take the children. The twins were sent to live in a foster home; Nathan came to live with a father he couldn't remember, a father he hadn't seen since he was a baby.

I wondered how the family would cope. The father had remarried. He and his new wife had two toddlers of their own and expected another baby soon. Money was scarce. They lived in a two-bedroom house in a housing development that sat in a sea of mud during Portland's monsoons. Yet his stepmother seemed delighted with this new addition to her family.

Nathan had never been to school. He was joining a class that had already finished a five month prereading course and was well into the phonics program. *He'll need extra help*, I thought. *He'll have to catch up if he's going to be happy in school.*

I needn't have worried. Nathan hadn't read the case histories that I had. He showed no signs of being a "troubled" child. He blossomed in school. If we expected him to learn, then learn he would. He tackled every project in his own serious way and was soon on his way to reading.

But he continued to grieve for the twins. I'd expected him to turn his attention to caring for his new stepsisters, but he remained aloof from them. He would have been a loner in school too, but the other students turned to him as a leader, and he helped them when they came. School was probably the first place in Nathan's life where his needs had been important to anyone.

Yet Nathan had a problem. He was a collector. I noticed that things were missing—puzzle pieces, scissors, crayons, beads, the small things that make up the equipment of a kindergarten. I supposed that the children were doing a sloppy job of putting things away and began to spend more time helping them during cleanup.

One afternoon Nathan's stepmother came to see me. "How do I handle this?" she asked. She had discovered a cache of kindergarten items in a closet. "He must be carrying things home in his pockets."

Together we decided that she would tell Nathan that the kindergarten equipment belonged to everyone, and it was to be left at school so that everyone could use it. Nathan would feel better if he brought everything back to school.

The next morning I watched as Nathan got off the school bus. He was lugging a big grocery sack. "I brought back your stuff," he said.

I was surprised. I knew that things were missing, but I had no idea that so much was gone. I felt totally negligent, but Nathan seemed pleased. As we finished putting things away, he said, "I'll bring back the rest tomorrow."

His stepmother and I laughed together when I saw her the next time. "I had no idea he had so much!" she said. "I don't know where he stashed it all in our tiny house."

Several points can be made concerning stealing by children:

It's fairly easy to tell when the child knows that stealing is wrong. Our neighbor's 18-month-old, for example, sees lots of things she wants when she comes to visit. She is very open about taking them, and she puts up a fuss when she is told to put them back. By contrast, a child who knows it's wrong will try to hide the item or will make up a cover story when questioned about where it came from. I'm not sure when this awareness of right and wrong begins, but I'm certain it's sometime before kindergarten. I've never told a kindergartner not to go through my desk, yet I've never had one do so.

Parents need to explain why people don't help themselves to food in a grocery store or to pencils in another student's desk. In families, where everything is shared and where children help themselves when they want something, this isn't as obvious as we might expect.

It's important for a child to return stolen items. Parents may need to go with the child, or talk to the person involved, but even very young children need to make it right themselves.

Begin early. Even very young children can be taught to take care of their own possessions and to respect the property of others. They can sort their own socks and put away their things. They can ask permission before getting into another person's things.

88 ARE WE THERE YET?ARE WE THERE YET?

Children must be taught to respect the property of others. They often don't see the difference between taking things and destroying property. If there is no penalty for running through a neighbor's flower beds, it can be an easy step to vandalizing a school building or taking property there.

Adult friends would do well to ask permission before giving a child something. That way, the parent knows where it came from and won't question the child about it.

CHAPTER 15

Shoplifting

Shoplifting is a form of stealing, but it brings a whole new set of problems with it. I first ran into this problem when I worked part-time in a department store when I was in high school. It was my first real job, and I loved it.

One day a girl I knew vaguely from school came in. Rich and popular, she ran with the "in" crowd. She hardly noticed me in school. Now, however, she seemed glad to see me. She even stopped to chat for a while. I wasn't flattered, merely puzzled, by the sudden change in behavior.

Later I learned that I had been a "cover" for her shoplifting. A clerk on the mezzanine had spotted her taking something but had been unable to summon help in time. I had been "had."

While many children—and adults—shoplift, few need the items taken. Many carry enough money to pay for them. Some offer to purchase the item, if charges are dropped.

Shoplifting is a *crime*, and children need to know this. Here are some suggestions for helping your child:

Keep an eye on young children when you take them shopping. They are used to taking what they want when they are at home. It's easy to follow the same pattern when they are in a store. If your child takes something, ask him to put it back on the shelf or into the shopping cart until it is paid for.

Be very careful about sampling the grapes or using an item before it is paid for. Children decide on their ideas of rightness by watching adults. Allowing the child to eat the candy or wear the shirt before it is purchased encourages the child to shoplift. Remember, the child may have forgotten the candy by the time you reach the checkout counter.

Teach your child how a store works. Teach him who owns the store, where they get the money to pay for merchandise, how clerks are paid, and what the profit margin is. Children often think that because a store has so much they won't miss the little bit that is taken. The truth is that shoplifting is big business, and most stores operate on a very small profit margin.

Teach your child who pays for shoplifting. Stores must charge more for their products to cover the cost of shoplifting. We all pay more because of it.

Teach your child about store security systems. These systems are a lot more sophisticated than they were when I worked in a store. Shoplifters are likely to be caught. Merely returning the merchandise is not enough. Most stores will prosecute.

Recently I was going down the escalator in a large department store when a teenager ran past me. She was wearing typical teen garb, faded jeans and a T-shirt. Her ponytail was caught in a rubber band. She was in a hurry. I looked around to see if a security guard was chasing her.

At the bottom of the escalator she whipped out her cellular phone. She *was* the security guard.

Keep track of what your children own and how much spending money they have. Insist that they get a receipt when they buy something. Be suspicious of new clothes or items that your child could not be paying for. Shoplifting is common among teens. I have found some junior high students to be remarkably adept at cover stories. "My friend and I traded" and "I found it" are common responses.

If this happens in your family, do not feel disgraced. However, you must deal with the issue or things are likely to get worse.

Permit your child to trade or accept gifts only with your knowledge. That way you won't be surprised when a store detective tells you that the lovely cashmere sweater your teen got in a trade with a friend was not, in fact, a trade at all.

Find after school activities that keep your child busy. Bored children can usually find something to do. Make sure that "something" is worthwhile. Look for Bible clubs, softball groups, music lessons, whatever appeals to your child. You may have to try several activities before you find the right one.

If you find that your child has shoplifted something:

● Talk the situation over with your child. Listen carefully, but do not accept excuses. Your child must accept responsibility for his or her own actions.

● Plan what the child will say when he returns the stolen item. Practice the exact words. It is important that the item be returned. This isn't easy for a child. I always worry that when the child takes the item back, he may be stopped by a security guard. Since he doesn't have a receipt, he may be accused of shoplifting when he's trying to return the item. For that reason, I think the parent should go with the child.

• Phone the store. Ask to speak with the manager. Explain what has happened, and make an appointment to see him.

• It is important for the child to explain what he did and to apologize. If your child is too terrified to speak, you may need to tell the manager what the child has practiced at home.

Let's hope that you find a manager who knows the right thing to say. You don't want him or her to browbeat your child, but neither do you want an "Oh, it's OK" response. It isn't OK.

Your child will probably be very tense when this is over. Any time there is an incident such as this—or any conflict between parent and child, for that matter—it is necessary to have a reconciliation. Your child needs to know that you still love and accept him. Tell him how glad you are that this is over, and that you are sure it will not happen again.

Look at the circumstances under which the shoplifting occurred and decide what changes need to be made.

• If your child was walking through the mall with friends who were taking things, perhaps the friends—and the mall—may have to be off limits for a while.

• If these are friends your child sees at school every day you may need to get your child into some organized activity to keep him or her busy and help him or her meet new friends. Swimming lessons or a soccer team might work. Check to see what is available in your area.

If the first you hear about the shoplifting is when a store detective or a policeman calls, consider these suggestions:

Your child, in this case, may be held by the officer until you get there. If not, take the child with you to talk with the officer. Sometimes you will be talking with a social worker.

- Listen carefully to what the officer has to say.
- Accept the penalties. Sometimes, if this is a first offense, the child will be warned and let go. If there is a penalty, be sure the child pays it, not the parent.
- Refuse to defend what your child has done. Your child did not shoplift because his or her family is poor or because you are a bad parent. He or she decided to do so. And that was a bad decision. The child needs to learn to make better decisions.
- If your child is underage the court will probably expunge the record when he or she reaches 18. Check to see if this will be done.

If this is not the first time your child has shoplifted, you will want to tell the child that this is a problem with which you both need help. Then find a counselor who will work with you.

CHAPTER 16

Helping Your Child Enjoy Church

Someone must have teased my father when he was learning to play the violin, because he carried on the tradition. He loved to tease.

"Put that thing away until you learn how to play it," he would say every time we sat down to practice on the piano.

We knew he was teasing, of course. No one learns to play the piano, or do anything worthwhile, without a lot of practice and many mistakes. Funny how we forget that when we're taking a child to church. This section is about helping the child enjoy the adult worship service.

There are many reasons for including the children in this service. The most important one is that children who are kept out of the worship service until they are "old enough" (able to sit quietly enough that adults are not "disturbed"), may choose not to attend then either.

IT HELPS TO LOOK
AT THE ADULT SERVICE FROM
A CHILD'S PERSPECTIVE:

- Children's bodies are growing very fast. They hurt when they must sit still for long periods of time. Their bodies are also very thin. When pressed against a hard bench, they hurt.
- Often their feet can't touch the floor. The circulation in their legs may get cut off, and their legs hurt. They are too short to see over the heads of the people in front of them, so they can't see what is going on.
- They vaguely understand the language, so the speakers aren't very interesting.
- The service goes on long past the attention span of a child.

HERE ARE SOME SUGGESTIONS
FOR HELPING YOUR CHILD
ENJOY THE WORSHIP SERVICE:

- Find a child-friendly church. You're looking for a church in which the members take seriously their major goal of nurturing the children of the church. Be enthusiastic about the church. When your child sees you enjoying it, he or she will see that there is something worth liking.
- Keep quiet about the things you don't like. Realize that no church is perfect. Take up problems with the church board, if you must, but don't discuss them in front of your child.
- Make getting ready a happy time. The secret is in planning. Lay out clothes the night before. Plan a simple breakfast. Leave the dishes in the sink and the beds unmade, if doing these things means a hurried rush to get ready for church. Children don't pay much attention to these things, and you can always keep a spotless house

when your children are grown and gone, if it's still important to you then. Happy times mean a lot to children. Neat houses do not.

- Teach your child what behavior you expect in church. Statements such as, "We sit quietly during the service," "We wait until after the service to talk with our friends," "We kneel during the prayer," can help. Be sure that you model the behavior you expect from your child.

- Go early enough to find a good place to sit. When our daughter was young, we found that she would sit quietly and enjoy the service when she could see the speaker and the singers. When she could see only the backs of heads, I knew I would be spending part of the service walking in the foyer.

- If the service normally runs past the time you can reasonably expect your child to sit still, sit near an exit. Most church services provide enough movement to keep the worshipers comfortable, but they are designed for adults. Services may be too long for your child.

- Take your child for a break between services. Many times the worship service is scheduled after the child has been in a children's class. Taking the child to the restroom and to the drinking fountain will help. If there is time, take a brief walk outdoors. Be careful not to make this break too stimulating. Running or roughhousing will make it more difficult for your child to sit quietly during the service.

- Encourage your children to take part in the service. Teach them the hymns and share the hymnal with them. (Even children who cannot read enjoy pretending they can.) Teach your children to kneel or stand when the congregation does so.

- Give your child something to do during the sermon. Very young children need a quiet toy or book to keep them busy. An older child might like a small note-book for recording parts of the sermon.

● Go to the social functions of your church. Attending church is a religious experience; we want to teach our children to worship. But it is also a social experience; we worship together. Your child will enjoy church more when he meets his friends there.

SOME CHURCHES DESIGN CERTAIN PARTS OF THE WORSHIP SERVICE FOR CHILDREN:

● Some design a special bulletin for children. It may have Bible stories or puzzles or pictures to color.

● Some pastors invite the children to join them at the altar when there is a baby dedication. The pastor reminds the children of their own dedication and of the vows the church members took at that time—vows to teach and nurture them in the Christian faith.

● Some pastors include special features. One pastor told me how interested the children were when he included a chalk talk with his sermon.

● Include children in the service. Some churches include the very young children in the first part of the service, and then invite them to another room for Bible stories and songs while the adult service continues.

In spite of your best efforts, you may find yourself, as I once did, sitting behind an elegant lady wearing a fox stole, complete with heads and tails and tiny paws. If you find, as I did, that your children just can't stifle their giggles, you may need to take them out until they can pull themselves together. Be very gentle in what you say about the behavior you didn't like, and even slower to punish. At such a time, you need to remind yourself that your goal is to teach your child to worship

God. Attending church is a good way of doing this.

One parent told of driving past her church during the week, on the way home from shopping. Her 2-year-old pointed to the church and said, " Spank!" Children who associate church with spanking are not learning to like it. Resist the notion that your job is to keep your child from disturbing other people during the service. You will find that most members are sympathetic with your efforts to teach your child to worship. Far from being disturbed, they are glad you came to church—and that you brought your child with you.

CHAPTER 17

Teaching the Bible to a Child

I've heard it said that there are no atheists in foxholes. I haven't met any in primary school either. It's easy for a child to believe in God. Everyone around him is bigger and more powerful than he is. It's easy to believe in a God who is like his parents, only more so. The difficulty comes in convincing the child that a great and powerful God likes children. Here are some suggestions for helping your child know God:

Tell them the stories of Jesus and His life here on earth. Until the child is certain that Jesus loves him, I would stick with these stories. Not all children believe that Jesus loves them as a person. If they think of God as a great big "something" out there, it will be hard for them to want to talk with Him. And that's what prayer is, talking to God as a friend.

Sing the songs that tell of Jesus' love. Songs such as "Jesus Loves Me" and "Jesus Loves the Little Children" were old when I was a child. The reason they have lasted is because children like them, and they teach what we want our children to know. Children love repetition. They will enjoy singing a song long after you have grown tired of it.

Choose Old Testament stories that tell of God's love and care for His children. Stories like Noah and the Flood and Baby Moses in his little reed basket are favorites of children. Most Bible stories about animals are popular. My own children especially liked the story of Creation. After studying "The Wonders of God's Creation" in a family camp, we spent many happy hours roaming trails, looking for the "wonders"—pinecones and small rocks to add to their collections.

Get a Bible for your child. There are many good versions of children's Bibles on the market now, many of them are suitable for even very young children. Some of them have beautiful pictures that help a child to understand God.

Dramatize your child's favorite Bible stories. I have two granddaughters who like to dramatize the story of Queen Esther. The story of Noah is also popular. And most children have enough stuffed animals to make the story realistic.

Seek the help of a child-friendly church. Parents should look the Sunday school or Sabbath school program over carefully to make sure it is teaching what they are teaching at home, and that it's taught at a level their child can understand. Many of us have found that this is easier when we have volunteered to teach or help in a class.

Look for Bible clubs, summer camps, or Vacation Bible School sessions in your neighborhood. Many of these run excellent programs for children. If you can't find what you want, you may find it necessary to start one of your own. Don't be afraid to start. You'll find many books to tell you how. And there may be other parents in your neighborhood who will help if you get it started.

Go to church with your child. It will reinforce what the church is teaching if your child sees that you think it is important enough for you to be interested too. I have, however, met children who have been sent to church without the parents and still have learned to know God. Beth was one such child. Each Monday, when she returned to school, she had a Bible story to tell her friends. Her enthusiasm was boundless. I didn't know her family and assumed they were a very religious family. One day I mentioned Beth's enthusiasm to her mother.

"Yes," she said, "she does like it. But I don't know where she gets that. No one else in the family goes to church."

CHAPTER 18

Teaching a Child to Pray

Children who understand that God likes children and wants to talk with them, want to talk with God. That's what prayer is, talking with God as to a friend. It's important to begin early, so that the child knows how.

Many times children have been praying along with their family since they were babies; they may not even remember when they first began to pray. But as children begin to understand what God is like, they will want to pray on their own. That's the goal we're working for. Here are some suggestions for teaching a child how to pray:

Teach by example. Parents who pray in front of their children have an easier time teaching them to pray.

Establish an attitude of prayer. Children are easily distracted. It's easier for them to pray when they can shut out the distractions. Folding their hands, bowing their heads, and closing their eyes may help.

Keep your prayers short. Be especially careful not

to ask children to kneel for a long period of time. They won't be thinking of praying if their knees hurt.

Vary your prayers. Families have tried different methods. Sometimes one person prays. Sometimes the family recites a prayer together. Sometimes a parent prays a sentence, and a child adds another one. In some families the parent prays a sentence, and the children add a refrain.

Use the child's own language. When I was a child, I thought that God spoke Elizabethan English. That was how people prayed in our church, and it was the language in our Bibles. That wasn't the way we talked at our house, and I could never get the thees and thous just right. I loved Jesus, but I didn't pray very much. Encourage your child to use the same language he or she uses when talking with friends.

Set aside certain times for prayer. Many parents pray with their children at bedtime, at mealtimes, and before the child leaves for school.

Jason was a boy who was very disruptive in my class. I tried all of the strategies I had learned, but nothing worked. I finally notified his mother that I was having problems. She seemed concerned, but didn't say much. However, the disruptive behavior stopped immediately. This wasn't too surprising; children usually shape up after a teacher talks with a parent, but it doesn't last long. Breaking old habits takes time.

But it lasted. When I told Jason how pleased I was with the change, he told me that every morning his family prayed with him, praying that he would have a good day at school.

It used to bother me that children sometimes understand prayer to mean asking God for something, and then begging until they get it. It's like Jamie, a kindergarten child, once told me.

He bounced into the classroom one Monday afternoon and said, "Teacher, I've been to church, and I learned all about God."

"That's great, Jamie," I said. "What did you learn?"

"Well," he said, "I learned that if you pray to Him, He'll go to the store and buy you anything you want."

That's a misunderstanding of God. The reason it doesn't bother me as much as it used to when I find children who hold this view is that I am coming to understand that none of us, adults included, understand God very well. Many of us picture God as the holder of a gold credit card. He'll give us what we want if we can manage to find the right way to ask or the right people to pray for us. That's why it is important to teach the child that God does what is best for us, and that's what we should be praying for.

The child should learn to talk to God about anything he or she would talk about to a friend. Some parents have found these things helpful when they pray with their children:

- Thank God for what He has given us.
- Pray for others.
- Tell God what's worrying us.
- Tell God where we need help.
- Tell God anything else we want to say.
- Tell God we want Him to teach us.

A friend of mine has a son who recently married a woman with a 9-year-old daughter. The child had not been going to church before the marriage, but now that she has started, she loves it. She reads the Bible with the excitement we wish all children could have. Her grandmother told how she begins her prayer: "Oh, God, you have so much to teach me." That's how we should all be praying.

CHAPTER 19

Talking With a Child About Death

The students were on their way back from the playground one cold January afternoon when a third-grader collapsed in the hall. We all knew that Joshua had a serious heart problem. He had continued in school while his doctors tried to build him up enough to live through the planned heart surgery. A teacher resuscitated him, and he was breathing by the time the ambulance arrived. But when the news rippled through the school that Joshua had died soon after arriving at the hospital, we had some tense and anxious children on our hands. When I talked with my class about it, the first question they asked was, "But he'll be all right, won't he?"

Children are used to television's quick fix, where everything has a happy ending. In real life things don't always turn out OK. Bad things do happen. People do die. We adults don't handle the topic of death very well ourselves, and we do a poor job of helping our children understand death. We cover up so well that it's almost as if we pretend that the person didn't die. No wonder the children watching us are confused. How do we explain death to a child when we can hardly face the issue ourselves?

On seven occasions I have had to help a classroom of students cope with death. Here is what I have learned:

Most children's first encounter with death comes when a pet dies. This provides the parent with a good opportunity to talk about what happens at death. It helps to let the child grieve over his lost pet.

It's important to talk with the child about what has happened. Children are often left with someone else when there is a death in the family. They sense that something is terribly wrong, but no one talks with them about what is happening, so they deal with their fears alone. They need to know that people do cope, that they are not alone, and that someone is willing to talk with them about their fears.

It's easier to talk about death when the parent has a personal understanding of God. Children can cope with death more easily when they understand that at death the person is in the hands of a God who loves and cares for them.

It helps to be frank about what has happened. Euphemisms such as "God has called Grandma home" or "We will go to the cemetery to visit Grandma," are confusing to a child.

It's important to use language that the child understands. Statements such as "She has passed away" or "She is sleeping" are easily misunderstood. Jesus spoke of death as a sleep on two occasions—when he restored Jairus' daughter to life (Mark 5 and Luke 8), and when He raised Lazarus from the dead (John 11). On both occasions Jesus was speaking to adults. And both times the adults misunderstood Him. Small wonder that children are confused. When children hear death spoken of as a sleep, they may wonder, "If I go to sleep, will I wake up?"

Children need to know that their words and thoughts do not cause death. The need for this has always surprised me. I once taught across the hall from a teacher who died during the winter vacation. The principal and the new teacher talked with the fourth-grade students and their parents, and we all thought that things were going well.

But then, a couple months later, a mother came to talk with the new teacher about her daughter, Linda's, distress. Linda, who had disliked the teacher very much, had at one point said, "I wish she were dead!" When the teacher did die, she thought she was to blame.

I talked with Linda. It helped her to know that the teacher had been sick for a long time. She had known that she would die from her illness even before this student was in her class, and she was at peace with the thought of dying.

Children need to be told that only in the resurrection will the dead come back. Contrary to what children are learning from television or from our Halloween practices, the dead do not come back as ghosts or zombies to haunt people here. The thought that they do scares many children.

Death is easier to accept when we focus on the resurrection. Death would be a horrible thing if there were no hope. The Apostle Paul said it best when he said, "If in this life only we have hope in Christ, we are of all men most miserable" (1 Cor. 15:19). Your child will be comforted to know that we will see our loved ones again.

Look up some of your favorite Bible passages and share them with your child. The only accurate information we have about what happens after death comes from the Bible. Some of my favorites are: 1 Corinthians 15:42-57 and 1 Thessalonians 4:13-17. An older child might also benefit from looking up some of the cautions against trying to communicate with the dead. Passages such as Isaiah 8:19 and Ecclesiastes 9:15 may help. Paraphrase if you need to.

Pay close attention to a child's feelings about going to a funeral. Some children are ready for this, and some are not. Parents can judge this better than anyone else. Very young children sense what is going on around them much better than we give them credit for. They don't understand language very well, though, so a grieving parent might frighten a child. It may help to have an adult friend sit with the child if the child decides to go to the funeral. The child can then be taken out if the service proves to be too much for the child.

Our children were 7 and 8 when my father died. We drove to Colorado from our home in Oregon and stayed with relatives. We thought the children were old enough to decide for themselves whether they wanted to attend the funeral. They both decided to go, but on the morning of the funeral, the 8-year-old was so distressed that he was sick. The 7-year-old played with her cousins and didn't seem upset at all.

Sometimes there is a family gathering after the funeral service. Some parents have found it helps to ask a friend to invite the children over to play instead of staying for this. If this seems like a good idea, but nobody invites your child, take advantage of one of those if-there's-anything-I-can-do offers. Most people really do want to help.

Many children find it easier to cope if they are surrounded by their own friends. For many this means going to school as usual. Be sure to notify your child's teachers, however. That way they won't be surprised when your child isn't gung ho about such things as decimal fractions for a while.

Part of the anxiety a child feels upon learning about a death stems from the same "It could happen to me!" awareness that hits all of us. For a child, however, death raises another fear, especially if it has been a parent who died. A child may then wonder *What if my other parent dies too? Then what will happen to me?* This isn't selfishness. Children are keenly aware that they can't live without adults to care for them. It may be helpful to tell a child that most people die when they are old, that children can expect to live a long and happy life. They need to hear that someone will always take care of them.

It is especially hard when a surviving parent has to deal with his or her own grief, as well as with that of the child. Some parents have found these things to be helpful:

- Get the child back into his own routine as soon as possible.
- Reassure the child that this parent will be there for him. This parent isn't going away.
- Join the child in some physical activity. I know one girl whose father took her roller skating after school. Another took his son to soccer games. The son played; the father watched. A mother takes her son bike riding. She told me, "It isn't my favorite form of exercise, but I'm sure getting to know my son."

Children, as well as adults, handle their grief in different ways. Some show their grief by acting up. It's important for adults to recognize this and to be patient.

We once had an eighth grader whose mother died during the school year. The boy's behavior changed radically after the funeral. Formerly a sweet-natured hard worker, he began to sass the teachers, hang out with the school bullies, and refuse to do any work.

As he was in middle school he saw several teachers during the school day. We recognized the change as part of his grieving, so we all worked together to get him over this. We did not scold or punish him for anything. We were as kind to him as we could possibly be. After about two months he came out of it and went back to being his old lovable self. But teachers can't do this if they don't know what's going on. It's important to remember that there's help available, and parents should ask for it.

It's hard when a family knows that one of its members is dying. Sylvia knew for months that her husband was dying from leukemia. During the months before his death all of the family—Sylvia, her husband, and Luke, their 14-year-old son—met with a counselor in a support group. The husband recently died. Sylvia and Luke spent the summer camping before Luke went back to school in the fall. Life hasn't been easy, but they're coping.

A period of grieving is to be expected. If depression or behavior changes persist, however, it's a good idea to consult a counselor or therapist.

CHAPTER 20

Self-confidence

leaned against the wall while I waited for my second graders. They had spent the past half hour doing crafts in another teacher's room. Now they were lining up at the door as they finished putting things away. Suddenly I caught the drift of their conversation. They were telling our new boy that his shoes were wrong.

"In our school," one of them said, "we wear sneakers, not leather shoes like yours."

I hesitated to barge into another teacher's class, but this was not permissible. Put-downs are not allowed in our classroom. They wouldn't be saying these things if they knew that a teacher could hear them. It's hard enough to be the only new person in the room without facing rejection from your classmates.

Then I heard John's voice. "Leave him alone," he said, "his shoes are fine."

The other students who had not joined in the ridicule, but who had not helped either, now joined John in helping our new boy feel accepted.

Most children don't ridicule others. They don't initiate bad behavior, but they seldom interfere when others do. What makes children like John different? Why did he speak up when the others were silent? More important, how do we encourage our children to defend their values against what they see going on around them? After we have taught our children what is the right thing to do, how can we be assured they will have enough self-confidence to do it instead of following what the crowd around them is doing?

Here are some suggestions:

Recognize that fostering self-confidence is not the same as encouraging self-centeredness. You don't want your child to be an egotist, intent on only his own interests. This is different from having enough self-confidence to stand against the crowd, if need be.

Accept your children just as they are. Some have strengths in one area, some in another. Be sure your child does not feel inferior because his grades aren't as good as those of his older brother or a neighbor's child, or because his skills aren't the same as those of others.

Encourage the areas where your child is talented. Sometimes this is hard to do when those areas don't coincide with our own talents. Rachel is interested in athletics; she likes sports, and she is good at them. The rest of her family is bookish. They take her to practice sessions and go to see her games, even though it would be easier for them to push her into more academic activities where they feel more comfortable. Doing so would not only discourage Rachel in sports; it would teach Rachel that her own opinions aren't as good as those of others. An added benefit is that her family is becoming interested in an area about which they knew nothing before they started following Rachel's development.

Go to your child's performances. Being there assures your child that you think what he or she is doing is important. Children work much harder when they know their parents will see what they are doing.

Help your child do well in school. I have already devoted a chapter to this topic. Let me emphasize here that a child spends much of his day at school. It is important that he feel accepted there and that he does well.

Visit your child's school. Meet your child's teachers. Tell them about your child's interests. Tell them what makes you proud of your child.

Respect your child's opinions. Ask your child's opinions about family events, such as vacations or holiday dinners. Listen to your child. Accept what you can and explain carefully what you can't.

Give your child a part in caring for the home. This means chores. If your children know that their work is important in the family, they then see themselves as important to the family.

Avoid nicknames that belittle your child.

Never amuse your friends at your child's expense. Avoid telling embarrassing stories. Enjoy cutsy baby pictures in your own private moments, but don't show them to your child's friends. He'll be embarrassed.

Avoid negative comments about your spouse. Your child is a part of both parents. Criticism of either parent is perceived by children as criticism of themselves. Divorced parents may find this especially difficult, but it's important to work at it.

Spend time with your child. We've gotten used to hearing that quality time is important with children. I agree. It certainly is. But it's impossible to have "quality time" without "quantity time." Children take their own time in getting to know you; you can't fit their preferences into a tight schedule.

Use discipline methods that respect your child's integrity. There will be times when you must punish your child for wrongdoing. Be sure that the discipline methods you use respect the child as a person. Humiliating or harsh punishment is usually resented. Be sure, too, that the methods you use can also be used when the child is older. If you have relied on physical punishment when the child is young, you may be left without an effective means to direct the child when he is too old to be spanked anymore. Remember that you are teaching your child to be self-directed, to be willing to follow what he knows to be right, even when you are not there.

Using these methods will not guarantee success. There are no guarantees in raising children. But children who are sure that they are a treasured part of their family are more likely to hang on to their family's values than are children who are still trying to figure out who they are and where they belong.